China on the Move

A Franco-American Analysis of Emerging Chinese Strategic Policies and Their Consequences for Transatlantic Relations

David C. Gompert, François Godement,
Evan S. Medeiros, James C. Mulvenon

Sponsored by the Office of the Secretary of Defense and Centre Asie Ifri

NATIONAL DEFENSE RESEARCH INSTITUTE

The research described in this report was sponsored by the Office of the Secretary of Defense (OSD) and Centre Asie Ifri. The research was conducted in the RAND National Defense Research Institute, a federally funded research and development center supported by the OSD, the Joint Staff, and unified commands, and the defense agencies under Contract DASW01-01-C-0004.

ISBN: 0-8330-3676-9

The RAND Corporation is a nonprofit research organization providing objective analysis and effective solutions that address the challenges facing the public and private sectors around the world. RAND's publications do not necessarily reflect the opinions of its research clients and sponsors.

Published 2005 by the RAND Corporation
1776 Main Street, P.O. Box 2138, Santa Monica, CA 90407-2138
1200 South Hayes Street, Arlington, VA 22202-5050
201 North Craig Street, Suite 202, Pittsburgh, PA 15213-1516
RAND URL: http://www.rand.org/
To order RAND documents or to obtain additional information, contact
Distribution Services: Telephone: (310) 451-7002;
Fax: (310) 451-6915; Email: order@rand.org

PREFACE

This volume is the product of a conference, jointly sponsored by the RAND Corporation National Defense Research Institute (NDRI) and Centre Asie Ifri and held in Paris in June 2003. The chapters in the report were written by researchers from both organizations and subsequently edited to produce a mutually acceptable consensus document. The resulting volume represents a transatlantic view of Chinese national strategy and capabilities and offers a common path for engaging rising Chinese power. Its aim is not to compare official French, European, or U.S. approaches to China, but examining the issues through the U.S.-French prism has facilitated analysis of how to develop the transatlantic, U.S.-Europe dimension of China policy.

This research was conducted within the International Security and Defense Policy Center of NDRI. NDRI, a division of the RAND Corporation, is a federally funded research and development center sponsored by the Office of the Secretary of Defense, the Joint Staff, the unified commands, and the defense agencies.

For more information about this report, contact Evan S. Medeiros. He can be reached by email: medeiros@rand.org. For more information on the International Security and Defense Policy Center, contact the Director, James Dobbins. He can be reached by email at James_Dobbins@rand.org; by phone at 703-413-1100, extension 5134; or by mail at RAND Corporation, 1200 S. Hayes Street, Arlington, VA 22202. More information about RAND is available at www.rand.org.

TABLE OF CONTENTS

SUMMARY

China and the International Security Environment

China's international security environment has changed significantly since September 11, 2001. Regions vital to China, such as South Asia, Southeast Asia, and Central Asia, have emerged as nodes of instability. U.S. global military presence has dramatically expanded, and U.S. willingness to intervene, where and when it wants to protect U.S. interests, is on the rise.

Following 9/11 and the U.S. war on terrorism, the tone and content of U.S.-China relations have changed dramatically. U.S. policymakers now talk about maintaining a cooperative, candid, and constructive relationship with China. U.S. and Chinese policymakers alike have indicated a strategic shift in their willingness to seek opportunities for cooperation and to manage traditional problems in U.S.-China relations.

Considering its strategic environment--above all, the strong position of the United States and the insecurity of regions of special interest--China has several basic options:

- Attempt to counter U.S. power politically, economically, and militarily.
- Pursue political cooperation with the United States in current circumstances while building Chinese military power with a view toward countering U.S. influence in the long term.
- Pursue long-term political cooperation with the United States while building Chinese military power.
- Pursue long-term political cooperation with the United States without building Chinese military power.

Of these scenarios, the last appears to be counterfactual, in that China *is* building its military power. As long as the Chinese economy remains healthy, it is therefore unlikely that China would abandon its effort to acquire military capabilities that match its political-economic status and regional security needs and also strengthen its bargaining position vis-à-vis the United States. While the United States may try to dissuade China from pursuing certain directions in its military modernization effort, it is unlikely to succeed.

The two most likely scenarios are lasting cooperation and tactical cooperation, with continued expansion of China's military power. The best available option, from a Western standpoint, is obviously for China to pursue lasting cooperation even as its power expands.

Chinese Policy Reactions to Changes in the International Security Environment

Chinese diplomacy has undergone an important evolution over the last decade. Beginning in the mid-1990s, Beijing's foreign policy began to reflect a more sophisticated, confident, less confrontational, and more proactive approach toward regional and global affairs. These trends are reflected in China's increased engagement with multilateral and regional security organizations, and Beijing's growing attention to nontraditional security challenges. These changes are likely to endure over the next several decades.

In recent years and especially after 9/11, some particularly innovative thinking about China's role in world affairs has emerged. Chinese analysts have argued for the adoption of a "great-power mentality" to replace Beijing's view of itself as a victim of the international system. In addition, these analysts assert that China needs to more closely associate with the interests of great powers, and that China as a rising power needs to pay attention to its responsibilities as a great power.

China has reacted in numerous specific ways to the recent changes in its international security environment. Beijing has cooperated with the international community in fighting terrorism, combating weapons proliferation, and in stabilizing South Asia. China has led an effort to foster security dialogues with nations in Central and Southeast Asia. In particular, Beijing has increasingly sought opportunities to cooperate with the United States in managing these numerous global security problems. Chinese leaders appear to have decided not to pursue "external balancing" against United States presence in Asia.

China's Military Priorities

The changes in the international security environment have had a profound impact on the threat perceptions of the People's Liberation Army (PLA) and its civilian masters, creating bureaucratic and political support for accelerated military modernization. For the PLA, two of the most important perceived changes were the rise of dominant U.S. military power, as evidenced in Gulf Wars I & II, Kosovo, Afghanistan, and Iraq and the evident desire on the part of the sole remaining superpower to use that military power to pursue a global unilateral agenda.

These changes in PLA perceptions have also significantly shaped the trajectory of its military buildup and rapid acceleration of equipment upgrades and doctrinal revision that had heretofore been relatively gradual. Beginning in the early 1990s and accelerating after 1999, PLA modernization was elevated from a relatively low priority to a core element of national policy.

The goals of this modernization effort are to fill niche capabilities with high-tech acquisitions from Russia while the PLA undergoes massive internal reform in key areas such as education, training, organization, and doctrine. More recently, two decades of wrenching change in the Chinese defense industries have begun to bear fruit, resulting in significant increases in the quality and quantity of production in aviation, aerospace, shipbuilding, ordnance, command, control, communications, computers, intelligence, surveillance, and reconnaissance technologies.

Chinese military modernization efforts are focused on three pillars: developing regional area denial capabilities, building a capability to project and sustain military power into the Asia-Pacific region, and upgrading China's current nuclear weapons and ballistic missile capabilities.

Looking to the future, the pace and robustness of PLA modernization is far from certain, given the monumental challenges faced by the new leadership in fostering continued economic growth, preventing a banking crisis, and maintaining social stability, among other internal challenges. PLA modernization will likely be sustained at current levels, barring any significant downturn in state capacity.

Long-Term Implications for the United States and Europe

China's economic and military power in Asia is growing, affording it a greater role in regional security dynamics. It is inevitable that Beijing's influence in Asia will continue to expand. This will eventually raise questions about China's long-term commitment to cooperative approaches to regional and bilateral relationships.

It is not yet clear whether the new trends in Chinese diplomacy and military modernization are tactical or strategic. In other words, are these changes temporary or enduring and how deeply have Chinese leaders embraced these new policies? The research in this report indicates that both China's increased engagement with the international community and its accelerated defense modernization reflect a sustained shift in Chinese perceptions about their growing role in global politics as well as the need for more and better military options against potential adversaries in the region.

There is no contradiction in this combination of a relatively accommodating foreign policy and stepped-up military modernization. But it does suggest that the Chinese are keeping open at least two strategic options:

- Following a helpful approach toward the United States and the West until the military balance is more favorable to China.
- Deepening and expanding cooperation with the West for the long term, while improving Chinese forces as insurance against military or political coercion directed at China.

Roughly stated, the first option is consistent with the logic of power politics, in which countering American hegemony is of paramount importance. The second option suggests recognition by the Chinese of the value of advancing shared interests through cooperative policies, somewhat irrespective of relative power positions.

Although the United States looms much larger than Europe, or any other power, in Chinese calculations, European policies can affect whether the Chinese lean toward the first or second of these two strategic options. To the extent that the Chinese believe that Europe is sympathetic toward the need to balance and constrain U.S. power, they may be more likely to indulge in such thinking themselves. If, instead, they see the United States and Europe coordinating their policies on matters of common interest, from the Middle East to global issues to China itself, the Chinese themselves may be more likely to see the advantages of cooperation, not merely for now but for the long haul.

The advantages of pursuing common U.S.-European interests vis-à-vis China therefore outweigh any gains that might come to either from seeking an exclusive relationship with China. The United States and Europe should not let their differences regarding China give Beijing the chance to play one side against the other. The United States has much to lose by excluding Europe from its strategy toward China, and Europe has more to lose than to gain by engaging China while distancing itself from the United States.

There is an obvious U.S.-European bargain to be struck: Europe should not undercut the United States and the United States should not exclude Europe in dealing with the emergence of China. Washington should do more than simply consult with Europe about China; it should fashion at least loosely common policies. In turn, by undercutting the United States in China, Europe would in effect be undercutting itself. With European support for a common approach, the United States could harness Europe's clout to influence positively China's rise.

To the degree that this reasoning prevails over triangular temptations, several principles regarding U.S.-European policy coordination on China follow:

- The United States should not presume that it alone can or should influence Chinese strategy and behavior. It should view Europe as an asset and partner, not a follower, in a strategy to deal with China's rise and integration.
- Europe should take care not to give China reason to believe that any reckless international behavior would be regarded with less alarm by Europe than by the United States or, worse, that European sympathy would permit China to ignore U.S. policy.
- Neither the United States nor Europe should let otherwise healthy commercial competition weaken their joint efforts to achieve their common goal of integrating China and to advance and protect their common interests in East Asia.

These principles should be applied in several concrete issue areas:

- **Taiwan**: Any daylight between Europe and the United States on Chinese use of force would be dangerous; ideally, Europe would signal that it would provide physical support if Taiwan needed to be defended.
- **Korea**: Obviously, the Chinese need to feel constant pressure to twist North Korea's arm. That pressure should come from both Europe and the United States.
- **Southeast Asia**: Continued Chinese moderation toward the South China Sea and Southeast Asia generally, despite instabilities in that region, should be encouraged by both Atlantic powers.

- **Human rights**: The Chinese might take note of any difference in European and American attitudes on the treatment of human beings, and they might even try to reward the more understanding of the two.
- **Proliferation**: The Chinese should be disabused of any impression that Europeans are more relaxed than the Americans about weapons of mass destruction and missile proliferation.
- **World Trade Organization**: Intellectual property and other issues involving China should be common cause for the two co-leaders of the world trading system.
- **Arms sales**: The Chinese know they cannot get adequate advanced military systems from Russia, and their own military industrial base is limited in its technological capabilities. As Chinese military modernization proceeds, the United States and Europe should guard against being driven apart over American security concerns about potential European Union military technology sales to China.
- **High-technology markets**: The United States should not seek to extract total compliance from Europeans on their restraints to technology transfers while using its political influence to deny legitimate markets to the same Europeans.

I. INTRODUCTION

From the vantage point of 2003, China is rapidly emerging as central to the global economy and international politics. China's economy has grown at the impressive rate of almost 10 percent per year for the past decade and is the sixth largest in the world.[1] Beijing controls the world's second largest reserves of foreign currency and recently surpassed the United States as the largest recipient of foreign direct investment. China's integration into the global economy will further accelerate with its recent accession to the World Trade Organization (WTO). Numerous key sectors of China's burgeoning economy, such as banking and finance, are being forced to open up and liberalize, regardless of whether they are prepared. Beyond economics, China is a permanent member of the UN Security Council, possesses intercontinental-range nuclear weapons, and has become gradually more active in a host of regional and multilateral organizations. Since 9/11, China has emerged as far more active in addressing transnational security issues such as counterterrorism and counternarcotics. By most measures, China has emerged as a major player in global politics and its influence will steadily rise in the coming years.

Yet, the growing salience of China does not ensure that China will emerge as a cooperative nation in regional and global politics. Chinese leaders are unhappy with the distribution of power in the international system, and these frustrations may increase in the future. In addition, China's growing importance to international economic and political events is fraught with numerous uncertainties due to the mounting social, political, and economic contradictions inherent in its development. Thus, China is becoming more and more relevant to the international community at the same time as its internal challenges are growing. Beijing's ability to manage these uncertainties will affect the broader global community.

For China, the uncertainties and contradictions are myriad. The Communist Party is trying to change its identity in order to stay relevant and credible to the Chinese people, lest it befall the fate of East European Communist leaders. China's social contradictions are manifest in the growing divide between coastal and inland provinces and the dramatic rise of violent crime in major cities. China's economy is equally fraught with uncertainties. The annual budget deficit is at an all-time high, government-run banks are essentially defunct, state-owned enterprises desperately need to be rationalized, and the emergence of major outbreaks of rural unrest threaten to create regional political crises. China's entry into WTO will exacerbate these internal dislocations and internal tensions, and it is not clear that the political system will be able to rapidly adapt to these contradictions, uncertainties, and challenges.

By far the most significant challenge that China's leadership faces is ensuring that economic reform, development, and growth continue. Yet, doing that will require the Communist Party to accelerate its gradual withdrawal from economic and social affairs in order to ensure the free flow of information and transparency that are needed for a market

---

[1] It is important to note that the 10 percent growth rate represents the official, announced rate and is therefore subject to scrutiny. Later analysis in the report addresses this issue.

economy to function efficiently. Yet, these very steps undermine the role, relevance, authority, and legitimacy of the party.

These numerous uncertainties and contradictions, combined with China's growing role in global politics, present the international community with a complex package of challenges. American and European policymakers need to be more cognizant of and responsive to the complex evolution of China into a stable and prosperous nation. U.S. and European policymakers need to encourage the acceleration of social and political reforms while not contributing to China's destabilization, an event that could precipitate instability in global markets and regional affairs in Asia.

Organization of the Report

This report is divided into five major sections. Section Two examines China's changed international security environment before and after 9/11 and offers a notional set of Chinese response options. Section Three analyzes China's published views on its international security environment, drawing from a wealth of primary source materials. Section Four evaluates new trends in Chinese diplomacy, highlighting Beijing's changing attitudes about its foreign policy posture and approach to multilateral organizations. Section Five assesses the Chinese military's view of its security environment and links these perspectives to identifiable trends in PLA modernization. The final section outlines a common U.S.-European approach to deal with China's emergence as a global power. The Appendix includes the list of participants and the conference agenda.

II. CHINA'S ALTERED SECURITY ENVIRONMENT

PRE-9/11 INTERNATIONAL SECURITY ENVIRONMENT

Whatever the Chinese might make of their security environment, an alien visitor (schooled in Earthly strategic affairs) would notice a sharp shift in that environment over the past three years---- a shift marked especially by increased international stability and boldness on the part of the most important country in the world, and in China's world, the United States.

Prior to 9/11/2001, the United States and Russia were on a collision course over U.S. intentions to field national missile defenses. The Russians were not alone in their opposition to the American threat to discard the Antiballistic Missile (ABM) Treaty: China and even U.S. European allies strongly voiced concerns. In parallel, Russia was adamantly against further NATO membership expansion, especially for the Baltic countries, and dismissive of mechanisms for NATO-Russian cooperation, which it viewed (not without cause) as mere placation. Russia was one of the champions, along with China and France, of a multipolar world system, a concept widely interpreted as a means to check and balance U.S. power.

The Persian Gulf, the main source of supply for China's growing foreign oil needs, seemed reasonably stable: Saddam Hussein was in his famous box; Iran was moving haltingly toward moderation. Conservative Arab regimes showed no interest in reforming, and the United States showed no interest in pressuring them to do so. Oil fluctuated around $20 per barrel. The Middle East peace process was stalled, but violence was low.

The Korean peninsula was relatively tranquil, the disturbance from the Tae Po-dong missile testing of the late 1990s having passed. The 1994 Geneva framework was still in place, if shaky. South Korea and Europe were making diplomatic overtures toward Pyongyang (over U.S. objections). Enough oil and food flowed into North Korea to slow its economic meltdown and avert a humanitarian nightmare. The danger of a crash landing for the Kim Jong-il regime seemed to be receding. Japan seemed content with the status quo -- always a comforting sign for China.

The new U.S. administration might have looked worrisome but not menacing to the Chinese. It had come into office averring a modest international agenda (other than its immodest approach to missile defense) and a preference for "humility." At the same time, it beheld China as a strategic competitor, though not inevitably as an enemy. Its initial review of U.S. global defense posture assumed that the only potential "peer challenger"-- possibly having both the capacity and the motivation to compete strategically with the United States--was China.[2] Relations were bumpy, not helped by Chinese impoundment

---

[2] Although the United States has been careful to avoid official declaration of China as its most formidable long-term defense challenge, it has recognized that U.S. forces might one day have to cope with a foe much stronger than such regional "rogues" as North Korea and Iraq. Too much should not be read into such prudent defense planning.

of a U.S. patrol aircraft and detention of its crew. Also, the new administration ended the declaratory ambiguity about U.S. involvement in the defense of Taiwan, saying that it would help in that defense provided Taiwan did not provoke a crisis by declaring independence.

In sum, regions of critical interest to China were relatively quiet; Russia and America were poised for possible renewed (if lopsided) strategic competition; the opportunity for the United States to pursue missile defense was unsettled; and the United States evidenced little interest in cooperation with China. Objectively speaking, China did not have a strong incentive either to confront or to accommodate the United States in any broad strategic sense, or any pressing need to make such a choice. It could keep its eye fixed on what mattered to China: economic growth, international trade, political stability (i.e., perpetuation of unchallenged one-party rule), and national unity (at least dissuading Taiwan from declaring independence). There was no reason to change its policies on defense: a relatively low place in overall Chinese priorities and an emphasis on power projection and anti-access capabilities on its Pacific side instead of forces on its land borders and strategic offensive forces.

CHINA'S WORLD AFTER 9/11

Politically, no one disputes the factual preeminence of the United States as the world power, and increasingly strategic positions and diplomatic actions are shaped in reaction to U.S. policies. For its part, the United States says it prefers coalitions, but it does not need them when it comes to military action. It has said and shown that it will not permit opposition in the UN Security Council (UNSC) to stop it from using force offensively when it feels justified in doing so--a sobering development from the point of view of the other permanent members, not to mention rogue states. Despite its expeditionary power, the U.S. homeland is vulnerable, and likely to remain so because of U.S. openness and global integration. Because of this vulnerability and the fact that new threats, e.g., strategic terrorism, cannot be deterred, the United States has explicated a doctrine of preemptive war since 9/11. The combination of (a) unmatched military power, (b) a newfound will to intervene, (c) independence from allies and coalitions, and (d) willingness to strike before being struck leaves the United States in a commanding but, paradoxically, exposed position on the global security landscape.

By 2003, Russia and the United States had not only resolved the ABM Treaty problem but also agreed to cut deployed strategic offensive weapons to about 2,000 each. The United States is now legally and politically free to develop and deploy whatever ballistic missile defense (BMD) it wants.[3] It is also free to keep thousands of additional nuclear warheads in reserve, leaving it with total strategic offensive capacity still orders of

---

[3] The missile defense capabilities the United States intends to construct remain unclear as of this writing. The Bush administration has elaborated a multi-tiered architecture to provide seamless defense against ballistic missile threats from short to intercontinental range, which would cover the entire spectrum of Chinese missile capabilities. Immediate U.S. priorities include multiple "theater-deployable" missile defense systems to protect allies and forward forces and interceptors capable of destroying small numbers of intercontinental missiles.

magnitude greater than China's. The combination of U.S. BMD and a reduced but qualitatively superb (i.e., accurate, reliable, and invulnerable) strategic offensive force leaves the United States potentially able to deny China a second-strike deterrent threat, which might be unsettling to the Chinese even though a U.S. nuclear first strike on China is unthinkable.[4]

Russia has not only acquiesced regarding NATO membership for the three Baltic states but has even entered enthusiastically into more substantive security cooperation with NATO. More broadly, Russian President Putin has signaled that cooperation with the West, including the United States, is central to Russia's future and Russia's strategy--a remarkable about-face from a prior Russian posture that had featured, at least rhetorically, a close relationship with China in order to counter U.S. power. What precipitated this Putinian conversion seems to have been a combination of the ferocity with which the United States went after the masters of the 9/11 attackers, Russia's support for an anti-terrorist (especially anti-Islamic-terrorist) campaign, the feeling that the United States might now empathize with the Russian approach to Chechnya, and a recognition that Russia's future required ever-greater integration into the West-dominated global economy.

To be clear, Russia has not become complaisant toward the world power. By joining France and Germany in opposition to the U.S.-UK invasion of Iraq, Moscow signaled that U.S. self-authorization of the use of force was more than it could stomach. While there has not been a sharp political backlash against Russia in the United States--U.S. public expectations of Russian helpfulness are low, and in any case France has served as the lightening rod--there is no question that Washington is disappointed that the post-9/11 warming in U.S.-Russian relations did not extend to Iraq. Some of the pre-9/11 Russian rhetoric about resisting American global hegemony is back, and it cannot be ruled out that Russia will try to exploit differences between the United States and "Old Europe" (Germany and France).

On the whole, however, transcendent Russian interests--joining the world economy, becoming a reliable source (compared to the Gulf Arabs) of energy to the West, combating terrorism, and fending off Islamic radicalism--make unlikely a Russian departure from its recent Atlantic tilt. Opposition to U.S. unilateral use of force shows that Russia has its limits but not that it is going to jettison its larger U.S.-friendly strategy. After all, what are Russia's options? The European Union (EU) does not represent a viable alternative to the United States as Russia's Western counterpart. And China offers little that Russia needs beyond a market for weaponry, or perhaps a market for Russian oil and gas. In sum, its diplomatic antics aside, Russia cannot afford to alienate the United States or to stir up trouble on its western "front." Putin's behavior since the end of the Iraq war suggests that he appreciates this. While the astute Chinese could not have seen Russia as an adequate strategic partner before 9/11, they might well have learned from Russia's shift since then that outright opposition to the United States is hard to sustain.

---

[4] With only a handful of quite vulnerable intercontinental nuclear delivery systems, China has probably lacked an assured second-strike capability since it first acquired nuclear weapons.

The recent trauma in relations between the United States and some of its key European allies could be more consequential than Russia's maneuvers, even for China. A U.S.-European rift could disrupt world trade, weaken global institutions the Americans and Europeans run (WTO, International Monetary Fund, World Bank, UN, etc.), and reinforce U.S. predilections toward unilateralism. Disagreement over Iraq has been no ordinary Atlantic spat; it opened a deep political wound and revealed the existence of a wide divergence in strategic outlooks between the United States and its European continental allies. Of course, EU solidarity suffered as much as did U.S.-European solidarity over Iraq, thus precluding unified European opposition or counterweight to the United States. In any case, European's awareness that having the United States as an ally is better than not has led Germany and even France to seek ways to repair badly damaged bridges with the United States. Notwithstanding the Atlantic split over Iraq, China can hardly count Europe as a potential strategic partner.

At the heart of America's global standing and its position in critical regions is its capacity to back its interests, responsibilities, and diplomacy with military power. U.S. defense spending has increased dramatically following 9/11/2001; the transformation of U.S. forces is in full swing; and the gap between U.S. military capabilities and those of others--indeed, all others--is growing. Far from backing away from its global interests and responsibilities after 9/11, the United States is more ready to take the offensive against those who would attack it.

Very small, well-networked U.S. forces overthrew the Afghan Taliban regime in weeks, scattered al Qaeda, and acquired a military foothold in Central Asia, next to China. A year later, two U.S. divisions--again, networked with plenty of information and strike capacity--defeated Baathist Iraq in three weeks. It is increasingly clear that the best any possible military opponent of the United States can do is to develop asymmetric responses, such as weapons of mass destruction, in hopes of raising the costs of American use of force and thus giving the superpower pause.

Despite their defeat in Afghanistan, Islamist terrorists have vowed to continue a global jihad against the United States and others who stand in the way of their millenarian goals. America's worldwide anti-terrorist coalition includes, among others, the EU, Japan, India, Russia, Pakistan, and Indonesia--whose combined population is twice that of China. The coalition appears to have survived the dispute over Iraq for the simple reason that its members have a shared interest in protecting themselves from the likes of al Qaeda. The struggle has already reached Southeast Asia, as signaled by the Bali bombing, but by no means is confined to Indonesia. The United States has made clear by acts and words that it will go after the terrorists. With the potential for trouble--whether terrorism itself or the U.S. response to it--in Central and Southeast Asia, Beijing also has found post-9/11 common cause with the United States.

Of course, the central theater in America's post-9/11 offensive against terrorists and weapons of mass destruction (WMD)-toting rogue states has been the greater Middle East. The Iraq war could have far-reaching implications. U.S. power, responsibility, and risks in the region have grown. Arab autocrats are under pressure to change, including at last from the United States. Radical Islam could flare up in the Saudi peninsula and Iraq itself. Yet, out of this turmoil the United States intends for stability and progress to emerge. Much to its detractors' surprise, Washington is pressing for an Israeli-Palestinian settlement. By planning to democratize Iraq and Palestine, to end the mullahs' rule in Iran, and to push reform among conservative friends, the United States has shown it means to effect political progress in this dysfunctional and dangerous region--a tall order even for the world power.

In East Asia, North Korea has abandoned its international commitments (the Treaty on the Nonproliferation of Nuclear Weapons and the Geneva agreement) regarding nuclear weapon acquisition and appears to be exercising its option to produce and deploy a nuclear force. Observing what became of Saddam Hussein, Kim Jong-il is willing both to talk to the Americans (to defuse attack) and to proceed with a nuclear weapons program (to deter attack). Although North Korea is believed to have nuclear weapons and could have the capacity to deliver them in a few years, the United States has found neither the will nor the way to forestall a fait accompli. America's approach is to multilateralize the problem without promising a realistic solution--its hope is that Beijing will make up for its own lack of influence on Pyongyang. Japan is hinting at keeping its nuclear option open. China must view with alarm the specter of toppling Northeast-Asian proliferation dominoes.

In sum, in the post-9/11 world:

- Regions of vital interest to China--Northeast, Southeast, and Southwest Asia--are smoldering if not in flames.
- The United States has the power and the will, with or without UN mandate, to intervene where it feels it must.
- The United States is free to deploy whatever missile defense system it can develop and to maintain a high-quality strategic offensive force with a large warhead reserve to ensure superiority.
- Russia is anxious but is looking to the West rather to the East for a strategic mooring.
- In the war on terrorism, the United States has said countries are either with it or against it and is encouraged that China seems to be with it.
- The United States has also signaled its desire to expand cooperation with China to dissuade North Korea from fielding nuclear weapons and to convince Pyongyang to abandon its nuclear weapons program. The tone of Sino-American relations is much better and the content is more cooperative than imaginable just three years ago.

At the same time, our observant alien visitor may wonder whether the Americans might be taking on more than they can handle, especially if isolated. Transforming the Middle East is easier said than done, if not a fool's errand. The denouement of the Iraq conflict could turn bad if the liberated/occupied country becomes resentful, unstable, radical, or fragmented. Expectations of implementing the U.S.-EU-UN-Russia "roadmap" for peace between Israel and a new Palestinian state could be disappointed. As noted, a nuclear contagion could infect Northeast Asia. In all these arenas, the United States could find itself with few unconditional friends, especially with its key alliance, with Europe, on the rocks. Its economy is crawling, and its budget deficit is ballooning. In the end, the United States does not have inexhaustible material and political reserves if things do not go its way and if it has little support.

The Chinese would be right to see key regions entering critical times, American power rising, the door to cooperation with the United States open, but American success uncertain.

CHINA'S OPTIONS

Considering its strategic environment -- above all, the strong position of the United States and the insecurity of regions of special interest--China has several basic options:

- Attempt to counter U.S. power politically and militarily.
- Pursue political cooperation with the United States in current circumstances while building Chinese military power with a view toward countering U.S. power in the long term.
- Pursue long-term political cooperation with the United States while building Chinese military power.
- Pursue long-term political cooperation with the United States without building Chinese military power.

Of these options, the last appears to be counterfactual, in that China *is* building its military power. As long as the Chinese economy remains healthy, it is unlikely that China would abandon its effort to acquire military capabilities that match its political-economic status and aspirations and also strengthen its bargaining position vis-à-vis the United States. While the United States may try to dissuade China from military modernization, it is unlikely to succeed. But what of the first three options?

Countering the United States

In view of how China's strategic environment has changed in recent years, a more extroverted China could be tempted to try to counterbalance and constrain the United States, lest continued growth and unilateral use of American power work to China's long-term disadvantage. An unchecked America could block China's emergence and influence in Asia and could intervene where China has critical interests: Korea, Southeast Asia, and, of course, Taiwan. Chinese interest in this option could be reinforced by a belief that the United States might be overplaying its hand as world power and overextending itself, as powers are wont to do. Beneath the surface of American strength, China may see vulnerability.

This option does not necessarily imply a confrontational urge or a crash military buildup on the part of China; the United States has too much military, technological, and economic capacity and too much diplomatic clout for China to be brazenly antagonistic, to challenge U.S. power at every turn, or to try to close the military gap. Moreover, a strategy of toe-to-toe competition with the United States could damage China's overriding goals of economic growth and internal stability. However, China does have the capacity, properly focused, to raise the costs and risks of what it perceives as attempts by the United States to use its power, politically or militarily, at China's expense.

In this option, China would need to keep its fences mended with Russia, India, and Japan, since its military and political power would be need to be conserved for rivalry with the superpower. Accommodation with China's three powerful neighbors would also keep open the possibility of a multipolar coalition. For that same reason, China could cultivate relations with Europe -- one of the world's two economic superpowers and a leading player in most global institutions. On the whole, a strategy of counterbalancing and constraining the United States is realistic and affordable for China *only* if Europe, Russia, Japan, and India -- or, say, three of the four--were sympathetic.

This consideration alone may be enough to doom such an option for China at present. The Chinese surely realize that not a single one, let alone all, of these other power centers is leaning toward or could be lured into a genuine, strategic -- as opposed to rhetorical, diplomatic--anti-U.S. alignment: Russia because it is at last coming to terms with the need to address its internal weakness; India because it is more concerned about balancing China in Asia than America in the world; Japan because it continues to profit, economically and strategically, from depending on the United States; and Europe because most European governments tend to be sympathetic to U.S. policies, despite the genuine tensions across the Atlantic resulting from the Iraq war.

A strategy of countering U.S. power militarily and politically could require very large overall increases in Chinese resources allocated to defense and other international undertakings, especially if it had no partners. Even with its impressive economic growth, China could fund such a strategy only by reducing social and infrastructure expenditure or by permitting the PLA to resume its business activities--neither one is an attractive course. Finally, as noted above, China and the United States have real and important common security interests--perhaps more evident now than before 9/11--that could suffer if China were to embark on a strategy of countering U.S. power politically and militarily. On the whole, this option should look unattractive to Beijing, which may explain why its current stance is generally more cooperative than confrontational.

Temporary Cooperation

China could also elect to pursue cooperation tactically and temporarily, that is until conditions indicate that a more competitive or countervailing strategy toward the United States is feasible and affordable. The rationale for this option is twofold: First, current circumstances are inauspicious for China to risk difficulties in its relations with the United States; second, those circumstances could change. For instance, the United States could fall back from its international engagement; or, on the other hand, the United States could assume a more confrontational attitude toward an increasingly capable yet undemocratic China. Moreover, China's economic and military capabilities could grow to the point that it could afford a more assertive stance.

In this option, China might still cooperate with the United States against terror and in Korea; neither help nor hinder the United States in the Middle East; and downplay the image of assembling some an anti-U.S. coalition, yet carefully cultivate Europe, Japan, and India. China could acquiesce tactically on matters of more importance to the United States than to China (e.g., Iraq), while taking a firm line on matters of enduring importance to China (e.g., Taiwan).

In parallel, it could build militarily to degrade the ability of the United States to operate forces with impunity off China's coast. Given the long lead times associated with modernizing military capabilities, the Chinese are surely not ready to cast aside preparations for the day when the United States is not so disposed to cooperate. The long-term threat to China could also include Japan, especially if Northeast Asian insecurity shatters Japanese power projection and nuclear taboos. And do not forget that the Japanese have shown great interest in ballistic missile defense, which the United States might be willing to help them acquire in order to avert a Japanese nuclear force.

While current conditions are consistent with all three Chinese options, the two most likely are lasting cooperation and tactical cooperation, with continued expansion of China's military power. The best available option, from a Western standpoint, is obviously for China to pursue lasting cooperation even as its power expands. This begs the question: What can the United States and Europe (France and others) do to encourage the Chinese to prolong and deepen the cooperation that has been evident of late? We will return to this at the end of this study, after having looked at trends in Chinese international engagement, Chinese interpretations of their security environment, and the development of China's military capabilities.

Lasting Cooperation from a Position of Growing Military Power

Lacking candidates to join in multipower resistance to the United States, and mindful of China's need for growth and stability, the Chinese may be inclined instead to expand and extend indefinitely their cooperation with the United States. After all, Chinese and American interests overlap from Korea to Southeast Asia to the Persian Gulf, and these are enduring, not fleeting, interests.

Apart from the specific circumstances that suggest value in cooperation with the United States, the Chinese undoubtedly understand that sustainable growth will both require and foster growing economic interdependence between China and America. The two economies are quite complementary: America the source of new technology and insatiable consumer demand, and China an engine of production with a seemingly inexhaustible labor supply. True, this growing economic interdependence constrains the United States as well as China, which might embolden the Chinese to be less compliant. At the same time, awareness that the United States has an immense economic stake in

China might cause the Chinese to feel that challenging the United States politically and militarily is not only fundamentally unwise but also fundamentally unnecessary.

Opting to expand cooperation with the United States for the long haul would enable China to avoid a massive military buildup and thus to concentrate investment on internal development. At the same time, the Chinese can be expected to continue to expand their military capabilities, especially those relevant to the United States and Taiwan--their most powerful potential adversary and their most coveted symbol of national unity, respectively. Military modernization is not incompatible with a strategy of long-term political cooperation. Indeed, it could be viewed as important both as a hedge and as a way to avoid having to cooperate from a severely inferior position.

III. CHINA'S VIEWS OF ITS INTERNATIONAL AND STRATEGIC ENVIRONMENT[5]

It has never been easy to ascertain China's world views. Once upon a time, China was a monolithic and opaque system. The foreign policy process, although it was the object of several books, such as the late A. Doak Barnett's,[6] was largely veiled by the central policy process and its arcane debates. Official pronouncements and ideology were dogmatic and often far removed from actual policy. Actual policy may have been so pragmatic and case oriented that it was also impossible to deduct from principles. A major policy choice, such as the Chinese decision to enter the Korean War in October 1950, has been made intelligible only in the 1980s, from the partial opening of Chinese Communist Party (CCP) archives and memoirs that revealed the internal debate at the top of the CCP and PLA, and also showed the amount of arm-twisting used by Chairman Mao on his colleagues.[7] What we know about debates on foreign policy issues--relations with the Soviet Union and Chinese attitudes at the beginning of the Vietnam War in 1965--was also mixed with domestic policy and factional conflicts.[8]

Today, Chinese policy and views are certainly less monolithic, but they are still quite opaque when it comes to top decisionmaking. The reform of the policy process and its degree of openness have come in stages. First, since the 1980s, policy pronouncements became more detailed and occasionally technical or transversal, and not only ideological or dogmatic in nature. Policy institutes and think tanks appeared, all of them except a handful of nominal "associations" under the direct authority of a leading government agency. Limited as it was, this change brought fact-finding and objective analysis to the forefront. Together with participation in international conferences and studies abroad, this created what Alastair Iain Johnston has named, in the narrow field of arms control studies, a "learning process."[9] that was going to filter back to top leaders. At the same time, diversity of views not being encouraged, what appeared in this new network of institutions was generally felt to be either quite representative or a fairly reliable predictor of official views on the same topic.

ARE PUBLISHED VIEWS AUTHORITATIVE?

China has now entered a second stage of evolution in the way it allows *foreign policy analysis to develop.* Not only is the circle wider, with for example a distinct set of Shanghai-based institutes and researchers gaining prominence, but there is more and

---

[5] Thanks to Christine Druhle for documentary assistance and to Régine Serra for help in revisions.

[6] A. Doak Barnett, *The Making of Foreign Policy in China*, Washington, DC: Brookings Institution, 1985.

[7] Chen Jian, *China's Road to the Korean War, The Making of the Sino-American Confrontation*, New York: Columbia University Press, 1994.

[8] Thomas Christensen, *Useful Adversaries: Grand Strategy, Domestic Mobilization, and Sino-American Conflict, 1947-1958*, Princeton, NJ: Princeton University Press, 1996.

[9] Alastair Iain Johnston, "Learning Versus Adaptation: Explaining Change in Chinese Arms Control Policy in the 1980s and 1990s," *The China Journal*, No. 35, January 1996.

more open diversity and debate among expert views.[10] This diversity of viewpoints and the degree of factual analysis that now surfaces in the press and in publications by major think tanks might in fact serve to further obscure the issues. Indeed, it is now impossible to infer from a single set of articles or views what the People's Republic of China (PRC) leadership might do or even think. Nor is it possible to second-guess shifts in analysis from changes in slogans or ideological pronouncements. More often than not, the "wooden language" that still appears in some of the media is just that--empty talk disconnected from reality.

This evolution is probably a reason why analyses originating in the PRC are still being treated with caution and distrust. The first level of skepticism concerns what is intended only for external consumption, as opposed to more "true" views for domestic consumption. Michael Pillsbury expressed controversial views on the deception game played by China's strategists. He made a strong case when he contrasted the views expressed in English by policy experts with their less widely accessed views in Chinese to the domestic audience.[11] The doubts extend of course to official presentations of facts. James Mulvenon, writing about the 2003 defense budget,[12] hints that the published growth rate--9.6 %, i.e., far less than previously--could be a stage prop aimed at international observers. This would be designed to allay fears of an armaments race sustained by China. The judgment comes from the noted expert who, quite rightly, earlier relativized the rise in defense spending since 1989 by pointing out the scale of underlying price inflation in China. Indeed, even the most basic facts and their interpretation remain quite debatable.

It is interesting, however, to note for example that some of the Chinese experts identified by Pillsbury later reunified their views along a strident, dogmatic line. For instance, the expert turned commentator Yan Xuetong, often discussing the field of Sino-U.S. relations, has been voicing some of the most aggressive public views in the years 1996-2000. Some colleagues have dryly observed that this may be because of new strategies in media positioning: Chinese experts, like their foreign counterparts previously, have discovered that taking a vocal and extreme viewpoint guarantees more media time and notoriety. Popular books--and this is not only the case of *China that Can Say No*--often take a traditional and conservative hard line that more or less consciously echoes 19th century geopolitical thinking, where possession of space and resources take precedence over any other consideration.[13]

---

[10] David M. Lampton, *The Making of Chinese Foreign and Security Policy in the Era of Reform, 1978-2000,* Stanford, CA: Stanford University Press, 2001.
[11] Michael Pillsbury, *China Debates the Future Security Environment*, Washington, DC: Department of Defense, Office of Net Assessment, 2000.
[12] James Mulvenon, "Reduced Budgets, the 'Two Centers,' and Other Mysteries of the 2003 National People's Congress," *China Leadership Monitor*, No.7, which can be found at: http://www.chinaleadershipmonitor.org/20033/jm.html.
[13] A good example of that trend was Ni Jianmin, ed., *Guojia dili:cong dili bantu dao wenhua bantu de lishi kaocha* [An Examination of the Nation's History from Geographical to Cultural Traits from Geography to Culture], 3 volumes, Beijing: Zhongguo guoji guangbo chubanshe, December 1997. Ni Jianmin is a researcher associated with the Chinese State Council.

Others--and the example of Americanist Wang Jisi comes to mind, or the example of Shanghai-based nuclear expert Shen Dingli--have on the contrary confirmed over time the consistency and the continuity of their views, while the criticism they undergo from time to time is a sign that they don't necessarily toe the line of their leaders. In short, nothing is assured. While in the late 1990s the trend among international analysts was to suspect a *maskirovka* at work in published analyses and data, today it is rather the lack of representativity of many analyses that might be suggested. The informed guess ten years ago was that the PRC was doing more than met the eyes (defense spending, missile and nuclear forces, long-term planning against Taiwan, and challenges in the Pacific). Today the same informed views would rather point out what the PRC is *not* doing in spite of what it says. Examples are the following: opposing the war on Iraq in word and deed, building up a Shanghai Cooperation Organization that has few proven concrete consequences, and working to improve China's position in a unipolar world rather than promoting multipolarity.

These episodes might be partially explained away by the growing sophistication and complexity of China's relation to the outside world. China spans the extremes of the contemporary relationship between the nation-state and globalization. On the one hand, its sense of sovereignty, enhanced by past encroachments; the continental approach that belongs to most ordinary and peaceful Chinese; its lingering nostalgia of self-sufficiency; and its closed bureaucratic process make it one of the few surviving nation-states that do not think spontaneously of regional or global integration. Together with food grain production--which has only recently lost its priority under a new WTO-oriented commercial policy--national defense and the perceptions of national security threats embody the most traditional elements of China. On the other hand, China is arguably becoming one of the emerging economies that is most interdependent with the outside world. Chinese technology, investments, trade, firm structure and ownership, and employment growth and mobility have become heavily dependent on global and regional integration. All of this might be taken as an argument in favor of a China "adapting" to the globalization process rather than "learning" from it. As a perceptive Taiwanese expert has noted, amid much praise, about David Lampton's edited volume on Chinese foreign policy,

> the volume--like many in the extant Western literature--uncritically accepts an artificial (and arguably false) dichotomy between China's so-called parochial, nationalistic, and unilateralist national interests on the one hand, and the cosmopolitan, transnationalist and multilateralist norms and practices on the other. . . . They fail to appreciate that the Chinese nation-state . . . is entitled to have a meaningful say in reforming or transforming the U.S. dominated architecture of global governance and in the construction of the prevailing international norms.[14]

---

[14] Chu Yunhan, "China Coping with Complex Interdependence: Neoliberal Institutionalism and Beyond," *Issues and Studies*, Vol. 38-39, December 2002/March 2003, p. 361.

The point here is not so much a particular doctrine or theory: It is to emphasize that beyond the degree of adaptation to international circumstances that China has shown in order to develop itself, there is no reason to assume that China's intellectual and expert elite will move from its previous nationalistic and ideological perspective to blind faith in the international system. China's elite is frustrated by the tide of "soft power" (Joseph Nye) radiating from America and the rest of the West and may well seek to rebuild a separate system of values and principles.

Mainland expert Wang Jisi, in his own elliptical and humorous way, offers a different judgment when he writes that upholding China's honor by defending a position of principle over the war against Iraq would have implied paying a far too high price.[15] A low profile is in China's interest, in his opinion, unlike for U.S. allies who can afford to dissent. In this case, one of China's most cosmopolitan foreign policy experts explains China's choice as a case of adaptation, certainly not as a case of learning or even less of shared values. A younger generation, often schooled in Western theory of international relations, flatly rejects its premises and predicts the rise of a "Chinese school of thought" in international relations.[16] In this proposed system, individual and institutional benevolence, altruism, interstate cooperation, moral international politics, harmony, order, and an open international system are juxtaposed against a Western international relation system that takes no account of differences in time and space and ignores other experiences.

Little of this narrative surfaces in the self-confident assertions of national security scenarios, or in the pronouncements about China's present and future economic path. Yet the two are often mutually contradictory. To start with the second, China's development is now heavily based on coastlines and dependent on ports, communication links, and financial exchanges. The old "third front" Maoist policy of developing the hinterland and central China is gone. Even China's Western development policy today is more a matter of regional spread in economic links than of building independent economic bases.[17] The PRC understands well the vulnerability of modern, concentrated economies, constructing exactly the type of arsenal to be used against Taiwan that could be used with a devastating effect against its own resources: naval interdiction, destruction of key ports of communication and energy stocks, and devastation of major population centers. Historically, dynamic economies with intensive foreign trade and long lines of communications have sought to defend themselves as far away from their shores as possible, developing colonies, then allies, then projection forces. What the American "blue" team expected China to do was a mirror image of what America, after Britain, did. Out of necessity perhaps coinciding with choice, it is not what China is doing or attempting to do. The modernization of forces has been largely focused on the defense of

[15] Wang Jisi, "The Main Characteristics of the New International Situation and China's Foreign Policy," *Xiandai guoji wenti*, No. 4, 2003.

[16] Yiwei Wang, "Between Science and Art: the End of American@IRT.com and the Rise of Chinese@IRT.com," paper for the 27th Annual Conference of British International Studies Association at London School of Economics on December 16th, 2002. Wang is with the Center for American Studies, Fudan University.

[17] See François Godement, ed., "China's Western Frontier," *Les Cahiers d'Asie*, No. 1, Paris: Centre Asie Ifri, 2002.

maritime approaches to the coastline, although elements of a real blue water navy are being acquired. Air power projection remains very limited, although short-range presence is more and more important. Bases and long-range logistics, including maritime or airborne transport of troops, remain quasi nonexistent. Two decades of South China Sea incidents and/or talks have not expanded the argument that the PRC was set on a project to turn the area into a Chinese lake. Is it possible, therefore, that the following interpretation might prove retrospectively true: While China underscored its military modernization and let it be known that it was seeking a capacity for projecting its forces beyond its borders, this program remained always subject to China's larger goals of economic modernization and rise?

This question is not to be taken lightly or circuitously. Recent international events--the issue of WMD in Iraq or even North Korea--have shown that interpretation is almost everything in identifying military trends, down to the very fact of possession itself. The lack of transparency on the part of the PLA has often been ascribed to a reluctance to uncover the Chinese army's weakness, rather than to secretiveness about its achievements.

Does this analysis extend to China's nuclear and ballistic forces? A core intercontinental ballistic missile force constituting a minimal deterrent is threatened by the imminent rise in ballistic missile defense programs by the United States and some of its allies, most notably Japan. At the same time the shift in military posture facing Taiwan since 1995 has coincided with the development and deployment in increasingly large numbers of short- and mid-range missiles of increasing accuracy and readiness. Today, China's most obvious strength lies no longer where its nuclear doctrine pretends to be--in a posture of minimal but assured deterrence, without need for a first strike option--but where it is not: in the development of a robust as well as accurate short- and mid-range ballistic force that could be even more dangerous with WMD warheads. Its existence literally begs the issue of a first strike doctrine. Formidable as it may be to China's regional neighbors, this force could never serve as a deterrent against the United States, or against India or Russia for that matter. Yet the doctrine--and the view of the world that goes with it--remains in place, and this new and far more imposing development is not justified by an articulate view or doctrine.

THE INTERACTION WITH DOMESTIC ISSUES

Open debates and a limited but real form of pluralism in the presentation of foreign policy views may also obscure as much as clarify the assessment of China's leadership views. Since the 16th Party Congress in 2002, domestic factional politics may also play a role. Former president Jiang Zemin seemed to win a complete victory at the 16th Party Congress and the subsequent National People's Congress session in March 2003: He kept the key position at the head of state and party military commissions[18], he stacked the Politburo and Standing Committee with his trusted followers, and he continued to receive foreign state dignitaries. The appointment of Li Zhaoxing (ambassador to the United

---

[18] In September 2004, Jiang agreed to finally relinquish his position as Chairman of the Central Military Position, his remaining leadership title.

States under Jiang's tenure), the outgoing Foreign Minister Tang Jiaxuan, and the centrist former trade minister Wu Yi to the Foreign Affairs Leading Group seemed to suggest continuity not only in policy line, but also in people. The central factor in legitimizing his position has been Jiang's relations with the United States in troubled times. Indeed, the spring of 2003 with the war on Iraq had potential for trouble, yet confirmed the Jiangist central path in foreign policy.

It is generally difficult to ascribe clear-cut foreign-policy views to several top leaders. Hu Jintao is no exception. He is sometimes thought to be more firm in dealing with the United States than Jiang; but that is only a function of his lesser past involvement in the compromises shared between the two governments. Zeng Qinghong, a very close Jiang Zemin associate, would seem to be tied to Jiang Zemin's general world views--which, by all accounts, include a low degree of respect for Japan. Yet, calls for a much closer and realistic cooperation with Japan have appeared recently,[19] which are described by an insider as speaking for Zeng Qinghong himself. Zeng has been side-lined from the Foreign Affairs Leading Group and also from the Taiwan Affairs Leading Group. For a trusted Jiang follower, to lean toward Japan is surprising, given Jiang's track record on the issue. That he would be excluded from both leading groups, after failing to show up in May 2003 at a reception of three major Japanese political figures he had himself invited, is even more eye-opening news.[20] Conversely, some of the choices apparently made by Hu Jintao and/or Wen Jiabao in personnel appointments are perhaps contradictory with the point of view of a further mellowing of Chinese foreign policy. The appointment of Li Zhaoxing, the new minister of Foreign Affairs and former ambassador to the United States, makes the point about the absolute predominance of relations with America over any other foreign policy issue. Yet his track record as a staunch polemist does not necessarily point to a more acquiescing China. Moreover, General Xiong Guangkai's mandate at the Taiwan Affairs Leading Group is not exactly a message of peace across the Taiwan straits.

Secretary general Hu Jintao, with no practical experience in foreign affairs, may have little elbow room and may in fact wish to reassess the strength of some Chinese positions rather than immediately leading an *aggiornamento* of that policy. There is no punishment for dogmatism, while liberalism can come under attack during a delicate transition phase. In a more lasting vein, he may combine Deng Xiaoping's heritage of reform with Deng's tough and realistic instinct in foreign relations. As a liberal reformer at home, and a Leninist and strategist abroad, he may have succeeded in emulating Jiang Zemin's centrist tightrope act.

Recent events in domestic politics include the following: a controversy over the official handling of the SARS epidemic; calls for more objectivity in media reporting and also for "serving the general public," while at the same time censorship is reasserted in some concrete instances; the reported dissatisfaction within PLA ranks over Jiang Zemin's

---

[19] Shi Hong, "Sino-Japanese Rapprochement and a Diplomatic Revolution," *Zhanlue yu guanli* [Strategy and Management], No. 57, April 2003. Shi Hong is with the Institute of International Relations of the People's University.
[20] Willy Wo-lap Lam, "Hu Now Leads on Taiwan," *China Brief*, Vol. 3, No. 17, 17 June 2003.

continued hold on the military establishment; and also a purportedly more sober behavior by government leaders under Hu. All this could conceivably have some consequences on party debates over foreign policy and the international environment. Recently, as we have seen a controversy over military hospitals and publicly announced sanctions being taken against navy officials responsible for the accidental sinking of a submarine, one cannot but wonder how Jiang's hold on the army can be maintained against these contrary winds, despite his anachronistic and widely mocked attempts to create of cult of personality for himself.

The change toward a call for more media objectivity regarding international events may serve the same purpose. Several key achievements of Jiang Zemin's rule have been undercut by recent international events. The strategic partnership with Putin's Russia, climaxing in summit diplomacy around the newly formed Shanghai Cooperation Organization in 2000-2001 and a joint Jiang-Putin declaration in December 2001, has been cut down to more modest proportions. A recent view on Chinese losses and gains under the anti-terrorist banner concludes that the Shanghai Cooperation Organization, first set up to counter American influence, has been put to sleep.[21] Russia's acceptance of dismantling the ABM Treaty and its change of views on missile defense are points where Jiang's diplomacy has been rendered null and void. Similarly, the West's military entry into Central Asian states completes the "encircling" of China that Beijing has always feared. The combination of the presence of U.S. troops, special operation actions, and strong influence over Pakistan also weakens Chinese influence over the areas from South Asia to the Persian Gulf. While Chinese foreign policy shows gratitude to the United States for restraining India and obtaining a resumption of Indo-Pakistani dialogue, trends also clearly imply that China's own policy of balancing India against its alliance with Pakistan is no longer successful on its own. It is not suggested, however, that the motivation behind the American restraining hand lies with China; rather, it is driven by Washington's need to preserve the Pakistani state in the struggle against terrorism. Large weapons sales to Taiwan--with even more being contemplated in critical categories--weaken the dissuasive capacity that China's buildup has against the island. Finally, North Korea's feverish search for an exclusive confrontational dialogue with the United States has weakened China's hand in eventually playing out a regional solution and using the situation of the Democratic People's Republic of Korea to broker further rapprochement with South Korea or even Japan. In all this, Jiang Zemin's track record would seem to be poorer than expected from the point of view of asserting China's self-interest. He has preserved peace with the United States and done his utmost in efforts to deal with a new, potentially aggressive Bush administration, but to what gain in the diplomatic and international arena?

The Hu era, now under way in spite of the dual-headed situation created by the 16th Party Congress, is on an ambiguous footing in the foreign policy field. On the one hand, transparency and open debate on international events are undeniably liberal turns that fit well with some expected directions of Hu's domestic rule. China's public opinion, always

---

[21] "Chinese Diplomacy Under the Banner of Anti-Terrorist Struggle in 2002:Gain or Loss?" *Ershiyi shiji huanqiu baodao* [The 21st Century World Herald], 2 January 2003.

vocal and ready to rise to a nationalist call, had another occasion at a display of anger with the war on Iraq.

IRAQ, THE LIMITS OF MULTIPOLARITY

The point in what follows is not to recapitulate the pros and cons of the war on Iraq, or the merits of the positions of various governments. Rather, and much more vividly than the international aftermath of September 11, this section argues that Iraq has been a turning point for international relations, a test for multipolar/unipolar norms and behaviors, and the source of a key change in China's view of the international situation and its own foreign policy. Indeed, the starting point for this might well be the window on Chinese world views that France-China relations occasionally offer. Through numerous exchanges of views, including a "track two" dialogue held over the last five years by the Centre Asie Ifri with the China Reform Forum and associated experts from Chinese think tanks, a leitmotif has been the Chinese expectation of a more independent, multipolar foreign policy with France. This applies particularly to the "one China" issue, to human rights, and to the eventual lifting of European sanctions, although it never seriously extended to strategic issues such as the future status of national nuclear forces. Chinese experts generally found it hard to understand the complex layers of Franco-American strategic cooperation, as well as diplomatic debate or conflict. Some of the more seasoned analysts speculated openly that the bureaucratic level of foreign and defense policymaking inhibited the political government level from expressing or putting into practice "true" views about multipolarity.[22] By the summer of 2002, after some disappointments among the Chinese foreign policy establishment about French behavior (and in particular the sale in October 2001 of an observation satellite to Taiwan in spite of Chinese opposition), several experts felt that multipolarity was not the operating concept of French policy, but rather an element of diplomatic language. At the same time, and more insistently after the October 2002 UN debate, the Chinese position on Iraq was taken for granted by France. What was needed to solidify China's multipolar course was a more clear and unified European foreign policy that would be mutually reinforcing with China's search for a more balanced world system.

As some like to point out, the situation has never come to the test: A second resolution on Iraq never came to a vote, and the PRC did not announce in advance its vote. Yet there are grounds for judging that while France took the most independent and multipolar position in its history, China in fact moved to a more explicitly and predominantly unipolar view of the world, seeking "complements" to this axis rather than a counterbalance. Militarily, Chinese commentators did not mince words about the advanced state of U.S. military hardware and strategy. Noting that victory came without the participation of the U.S. 4th division, the most digitized army unit, Senior Colonel Zhang Zhaozhong of the Chinese National Defense University explained to the general public that although the "people's war" is not a dead concept, "it must change with the times." Military strategy, according to the commentators, now rests on computerized hardware and army corps, on "the country's scientific and technological basis," and "it must seek to protect the national strategic potential." In this type of war, the Chinese are

---

[22] Interviews in Beijing, September 1999.

not sanguine about their own prospects, arguing "many countries have difficult times ahead when they will become targets of an attack by the U.S. Army."[23] Gone in these judgments are the past skepticism about the U.S. will to fight or to sustain losses, or the talk about asymmetric threats. In fact, Colonel Zhang suggests fairly openly that defending national assets is already a difficult goal for the PLA.

Politically, the Iraq intervention and its legitimacy have reportedly been the objects of some intra-party debate. It is probably worth mentioning that the influential *Nanfang Zhoumo* weekly printed a call for political democracy by one of Mao's former secretaries, as well as a pro-war text, while Qinghua University, a cradle for China's new technocratic leaders, published an anti-war petition initiated by an anti-WTO activist.[24] Even the level of official criticism, at any time during the Iraqi crisis, has been much more subdued than over Kosovo in 1999.

Strategically, the stated or unstated goals of the war are taken seriously, and positive consequences are sometimes mentioned. An article intended for general consumption asks rhetorically: "Was the war on Iraq worth the effort?" Clearly, the expected answer is yes. Some argued that the strategic control of oil fields is vital for all industrialized countries. Others averred that strategic control will uproot anti-American terrorism and lead to a "strategic triangle" with Israel and Turkey. Side profits included a short-lived drop in world oil prices.[25] In sum, American policy "was not looking after a fake reputation, but seeking realistic goals."[26] Nowhere to be seen, of course, was the prediction of an American decline, although there are any number of dark but unspecified predictions about the perils that await U.S. troops in post-war Iraq.

Some analysts have gone one step farther. Feng Zhongping, in charge of European affairs at the China Institute for Contemporary International Affairs (CICIR), the think tank usually associated with the Ministry of State Security, saw the transatlantic division over Iraq as mainly about multilateralism. Europeans did not really differ from the U.S. strategic vision, but served to mitigate it, along with "American moderates." The real division was between a "Blairist" and a "Gaullist" approach among Europeans. Feng Zhongping saw China on the "Blairist" side of the issue: "Can we say that we stand alongside France and Germany against the UK and Eastern European countries that support a unipolar world? The answer is no." Why? Fang argued that Tony Blair had been more effective than others to mitigate unilateralism. Furthermore, the rhetorical European "counterweight" would likely fail to materialize, because European voters would not approve the necessary large defense budget increases. Transatlantic dialogue would go on, leading to a "unilateralism and a half" under U.S. leadership.[27]

---

[23] Interview of Senior Col. Zhang Zhaozhong, Internet edition of the *People's Daily*, 18 April 2003. Zhang is the head of the Center for Military Science and Technology at the National Defense University.

[24] Written by Han Deqiang, the text was handed to the U.S. embassy on 18 February 2003.

[25] It is probably worth noting that a consumer protest against the war had earlier been publicized over the sina.com site, protesting the fact that the cost of the U.S. war would be paid for by an increase in oil prices.

[26] All quotes from the *People's Daily*, 18 April 2003.

[27] Feng Zhongping, "Thoughts on the Relation of European Countries to the United States," *Xiandai guoji guanxi* [Contemporary International Relations], No. 4, 2003.

A perceptive expert might regard Fang's argument as representing a fringe view, but it was published nonetheless in an authoritative review. It is probably worth noting, in this context, that the PRC's most frequent interlocutor mentioned during the 21 days of open war by the spokesman for the Ministry of Foreign Affairs was Jack Straw, the UK Foreign Secretary. Other PRC analysts issued a more cautious analysis. Wang Jisi, for instance, publicly advised the Chinese government to "resist calls to behave as a responsible power as the price to pay for its own international rise." Rather, China was to establish good relations over the Eurasian continent in order to gain a long respite, since focusing on a good ending for the North Korean nuclear crisis was the first priority.[28]

A Chinese expert underlined another positive strategic consequence related to South Asia. India had long considered that the "pre-emptive war" notion in American doctrine would one day serve its own goals facing Pakistan. After the Iraqi war, the Vajpayee government was "woken from its dream." It had to take into account American pressure for a settlement of the Kashmir issue and had suddenly adopted a positive attitude of negotiation with Pakistan.[29] Such kudos toward American policy over India are very rare indeed, since a commonly shared view of Chinese analysts has been that India was a pawn in Soviet hands then was wooed over by the United States in an attempt to encircle the PRC.

Suddenly, in fact, the view expressed above by Wang Jisi appears conservative in the Beijing debate among experts. In the same issue of *Zhanlue yu guanli*, there were arguments in favor of a more proactive, pragmatic Chinese foreign policy that would be commensurate with China's present state of integration into global affairs.

CONCLUSION: STRATEGIC REALISM WITHOUT DOGMA

Evidently, China's world views have changed more over the last two years than during the preceding two decades of the reform era. No longer does one see a strategic classification of countries according to ideology or world order. There is no more a "three worlds theory," little mention of multipolarity, little mention of friendship, and other moral categorizations. Where morals reappear, it is in the realm of contemporary international relations, not along the lines of Maoist ideology. A recent analysis on China's relations with the so-called Third World is particularly revealing.[30] China now gives priority to its relations with "rich countries." The author further argues that it is contradictory to reach for an economically advanced status while maintaining that China is a developing country and that it should not, for example, participate in G-8 activities. As a result, the five principles of peaceful coexistence are no longer a realistic basis for dealing with the Third World, and China should not uphold the abstract notion of equality between countries. Within Southeast Asia, the article asserts, China has already broken

---

[28] Wang Jisi, "Main Characteristics of the New Situation and Chinese Diplomacy," *Xiandai guoji guanxi*, No. 4, 2003.

[29] Shi Chunyu, "Reasons Behind the Moderation of Indo-Pakistani Relations," *Dagongbao*, Hong Kong, 25 April 2003 (translated by FBIS).

[30] All quotes and ideas in the paragraph are from Shi Yinhong, "China's External Difficulties and the Challenges for the New Leadership," *Zhanlue yu guanli*, No. 3, 2003.

down its approach according to the development level of its partners and should do so all over the world. Beijing's main partners should be the fastest emerging countries, and it should also prioritize its action toward its neighbors, and toward countries that are strategically important. Moreover, to convince advanced countries of its morality and rectitude, the author argues that China should stop supporting, in the name of Third World solidarity, governments that oppress their own people. Finally, the article concludes that regionalization is the path of world integration, and China should follow that path.

Geographically, the main division is between China's neighbors and more distant nations. At a time when Chinese views and stands become more articulate and influential in world affairs, this is also a recognition that China's real influence does not extend beyond its immediate environment. There is pride in some new international diplomatic capacity-- such as the PRC's special envoy to the Middle East, or the potential development of the Association of Southeast Asian Nations (ASEAN) 10 plus One dialogue with China (still preferred to the wider dialogue including Japan and Korea). Russia is a partner that is important at several levels, including energy security. But a strategic calculus based on common stands seems to have disappeared from public expression. Interestingly, Europe is the comparative subject of much of China's domestic reporting of its evolving politics and society. Even more so than in the United States, Chinese views seem to be fascinated by the complexity of Europe's internal debates on foreign policy, and by the role played by public opinion. Regarding the United States, by contrast, the Chinese elites assert that the Bush administration seems to have suppressed most public debate.

While relations with European countries are mostly good, it is the issue of how to deal with American power that is uppermost in the minds of the Chinese. And more often than not, the challenge is not "dancing with the wolves," as Jiang Zemin is reported to have said in 1999, but how to enhance Chinese interests in a quasi-unipolar world. Shi Yinhong views the necessary rapprochement with Japan as an "indirect strategy" toward the United States.[31] He describes the two foreign policy directives reportedly issued by the 16th Party Congress as "implementing more firmly and patiently moderate views," and "pursuing military modernization while not tolerating Taiwan independence." While the allusion to what was perhaps previous "wobbling" is damning, strength is still the main focus. In all this, China is not departing from its legendary international realism. It is sticking to it and perhaps, indeed, "adapting" much more than "learning" about changes in the international system. The diplomatic conditions to maintain China's economic rise and the absolute predominance of the United States in the world are the main drivers. Yet more and more analysts in the spring of 2003, which witnessed a renewed political debate in China, also discussed the norms of the international system and, therefore, propose a deeper and wider Chinese participation in its workings.

---

[31] Ibid.

IV. A NEW ERA FOR CHINESE FOREIGN POLICY?

It is trite but true to point out that China is still changing after more than 20 years of what Chinese sloganeers call *gaige kaifeng* or "reform and openness." China's senior leadership is in the opening innings of yet another profound and intriguing political transition. The developments at the November 2002 16th Party Congress and March 2003 National People's Congress suggest an initial movement toward intra-party reform and slightly more regularized processes of political transition, though China still has a long march ahead on both fronts.[32] Jiang Zemin's September 2004 decision to relinquish his post as head of the military indicates further movement on this front. China's economy continues to grapple with the multiple challenges a decaying health care system, a functionally bankrupt banking sector, inefficient state owned enterprises, a ballooning budget deficit, massive unemployment, and growing social unrest in rural areas.[33] The Communist Party itself faces a crisis of governance in staying relevant and credible in a time of accelerating economic and social transformation.[34]

These well-known domestic changes and challenges are matched by an equally important, though more subtle, transformation in Chinese foreign policy. Compared with the early 1990s, a sea change in the *content, character,* and *execution* of China's diplomacy has occurred and is continuing. Beginning in the mid-1990s, Beijing's foreign policy began to reflect a more active, confident, and less confrontational approach toward regional and global affairs. These trends are reflected in numerous, gradual changes in Chinese diplomacy. More recently and especially after 9/11, some particularly innovative thinking about China's role in world affairs has emerged. As a result, China's approach to regional and global affairs increasingly reflects a growing sophistication and a limited degree of proactivity. These recent changes combined with the earlier shifts that emerged in the mid-1990s have resulted from changes in Chinese perceptions of the international security environment and broadening conceptions of Chinese national interests. These correlations of shifting perceptions and changing policies raises important question about which changes in Chinese diplomacy are enduring and which are likely to be more temporary.

The notion of evolution and change in China's worldview and its foreign policies may seem outdated to experienced China watchers and overly optimistic to casual observers of late. Yet during the 1980s and 1990s as China opened to the world, China specialists rightly highlighted the expansion of Chinese foreign policy interests and its burgeoning engagement with the international community in new forums, and on a variety of novel (to China) security, economic, and political issues. Little new work on China's *overall*

---

[32] See Joseph Fewsmith, "The 16th Party Congress: Implications for Understanding Chinese Politics," *China Leadership Monitor*, No. 5, Hoover Institution Stanford University, Winter 2003; Joseph Fewsmith, "The Sixteenth National Party Congress: The Succession that Didn't Happen," *The China Quarterly*, March 2003, pp. 1-16.

[33] Nicholas Lardy, *China's Unfinished Economic Revolution*, Washington, DC: Brookings Institution Press, 1998; Nicholas Lardy, *Integrating China into the Global Economy*, Washington, DC: Brookings Institution Press, 2002.

[34] Minxin Pei, "China's Governance Crisis," *Foreign Affairs*, September/October 2002.

foreign policy strategy has been done since these arguments were put forward.[35] Moreover, casual observers of Asian affairs have recently argued that Beijing's apparently "limited" involvement in the Iraq and North Korea crises indicates the persistence of traditionally passive involvement in world affairs. These analysts maintain that Chinese leaders continue to adhere to a conservative approach to foreign policy that involves taking as little action as possible to maximize Chinese interests, free-riding on U.S. policymaking, and all the while claiming to inhabit a sanctimonious moral high ground.[36]

This section rejects these lines of analyses. Beyond these somewhat jaded and cursory views of Chinese diplomacy lies the undeniable reality that in the last ten years Chinese foreign policy has become far more sophisticated, confident, and in some instances proactive. These changes have been slow and subtle, but from the vantage point of 2003, they collectively represent a substantial transition from the early 1990s. Chinese leaders have begun to cast off the shadow of a reactive nation reluctant to fully engage the international community in multiple forums and on a wide range of topics. Chinese strategists have gradually recognized the value to Chinese interests of active participation in regional and multilateral forums and addressing the full complement of transnational issues. Chinese policymakers have also moved away from viewing much of their foreign policy through the prism of the Taiwan issue.

Not only has China's participation in international debates and institutions increased but the quality of its participation has improved as well. To a limited extent, the Chinese are beginning to play a role in shaping the evolution of the rules and functions of regional multilateral organizations. In many ways, this shift in Chinese thinking and policies represents one of the most profound transitions in China's foreign policy since the founding of the PRC in 1949. These developments raise serious implications for the future of U.S.-China relations as well as the full complement of transnational security, economic, and social challenges confronting the international community.

This section begins with a brief overview of the historical developments in Chinese foreign policy since the Maoist era. This is necessary context for understanding the significance of the changes in Chinese diplomacy. The next subsection outlines the main arguments about the shifts in the content, character, and execution in Chinese foreign policy. A third subsection briefly raises some of the newest and most innovative lines of

---

[35] The subfield of Chinese foreign policy studies has become highly specialized in the last ten years. This is not to say that high-quality research and analysis is not occurring but rather that the proliferation of new data on Chinese foreign affairs has led scholars to focus on specific aspects of Chinese diplomacy such as decisionmaking, subregional affairs, China's bilateral relations, China and multilateral organizations, and arms control and nonproliferation. These fine-grained analyses have come at the expense of broad examinations of changes in China's overall diplomatic strategies. The claims in this section are meant to provide a new context for interpreting the excellent research on specific aspects of Chinese foreign policy. See Elizabeth Economy and Michael Oksenberg, eds., *China Joins the World: Progress and Prospects*, New York, NY: Council on Foreign Relations Press, 1999; David M. Lampton, ed., *The Making of Chinese Foreign and Security Policy in the Era of Reform*, Stanford, CA: Stanford University Press, 2001.
[36] Steve Tsang, "China's Failure in Diplomacy," *Far Eastern Economic Review*, 27 February 2003.

thinking in China about its role in global affairs. A final subsection offers some preliminary observations about the implications of these trends.

REBUILDING THE DRAGON: CHANGES IN CHINESE FOREIGN POLICY FROM MAO TO DENG

The first major transition in Chinese foreign policy occurred after Mao's death and the ascension of Deng Xiaoping as China's paramount leader. Mao's foreign policy was noted for its revolutionary fervor and bombastic language, its strong opposition to the "superpowers," its close association with developing countries, its relative isolation from international organizations, its economic autarky, and a general effort to oppose most aspects of an international system. In short, Mao rejected the structure and operation of the international system of the 1950s, 1960s, and 1970s and, at least rhetorically, sought to overthrow it.[37]

Beginning in the late 1970s, Deng initiated a dedicated effort to replace Mao's ideologically motivated and revisionist foreign policy with a more pragmatic one focused on integrating China into the international community. Chinese scholars characterize the shift from Mao's to Deng's diplomatic strategy as a five-part transition from

- revolutionary to state diplomacy
- anti-system to "participation" diplomacy
- simple "enemies, ourselves, and friends" diplomacy to "all-round diplomacy"
- choosing either one or the other between the U.S. and Soviet superpowers to the diplomacy of acting independently and making China's own decisions
- the diplomacy of the principle of safety first to attaching importance to economic diplomacy and so-called "low position" (*di wei*) diplomacy.[38]

For Deng, China's foreign policy was meant to directly, uniformly, and singularly serve the goal of Chinese economic development. Whereas Mao rejected many of the rules, norms, and institutions of modern international relations, Deng carefully began to incorporate some of them into China's new world view. Perhaps most important, Deng revised Mao's view on the inevitability of a major war among the great powers and declared that "peace and development" (*heping yu fazhan*) were the trends of the times. Acceptance of this critical slogan persists today, and internal debates on it serve as a critical bellwether of Chinese views on international stability.[39]

---

[37] For details on these views, see the classic texts of Michael Yahuda, *China's Role in World Affairs*, New York, NY: St Martin's Press, 1978; and Michael Yahuda, *Towards the End of Isolationism: China's Foreign Policy After Mao*, New York, NY: St. Martin's Press, 1983.

[38] Li Limin, "Zhauzhu jiyu, jueding hao Zhongguo yu shijie de guanxi [Seizing Good Fortune and Resolving China's Relations with the World]," *Xiandai guoji guanxi*, No. 4, 2003, pp. 24-26.

[39] David M. Finkelstein, *China Reconsiders Its National Security: The Great Peace and Development Debate of 1999*, Washington, DC: CNA Corporation, December 2000. Also see Denny Roy, "China's Pitch for a Multipolar World: The New Security Concept," Honolulu, HI: Asia-Pacific Center for Security Studies, Volume 2, May 2003.

In the 1980s, China focused on building its relations with the United States, Japan, and European countries in order to balance the Soviet threat and to gain access to trade and foreign direct investment. Although Beijing's foreign policy remained rhetorically "independent," Deng had clearly realigned China's core foreign policy interests away from an exclusive focus on developing nations and toward building relations with leading economic powers. At the same time, China sought to expand its international profile by significantly increasing its participation in intergovernmental and nongovernmental organizations alike. Deng's foreign policy successfully initiated the long and gradual process of extracting China from Mao-era isolation.

However, Deng's efforts to revamp China's diplomatic work had real limitations. Although China's formal participation in international organizations nominally expanded, Chinese delegates seldom contributed substantively to the organizations' work. The lack of quality participation on the part of China was similarly reflected in the foreign policy decisionmaking and public relations apparatus. Under Deng, policymaking on foreign affairs and national security issues remained relatively centralized (though less so than in the Mao era) and the purview of a small coterie of senior CCP leaders. China's diplomatic core was small, under-trained and inexperienced because the Foreign Ministry had suffered particularly acute pains during the Cultural Revolution. In addition, Beijing did a poor job of articulating and communicating its world views. China often couched Deng's pragmatic and integrationist policies in oblique socialist rhetoric that made it difficult for many, save dedicated sinologists, to understand Chinese policies and to discern them from China's actual practices. Beijing offered little transparency about its policies beyond boilerplate foreign ministry and CCP formulations, and these were not well circulated or publicized. Even Chinese international relations journals offered literally nothing more than the precise CCP line with only the faintest hint of independent analysis and insight.[40]

CHINA'S MORE FLEXIBLE DIPLOMACY

These limitations in China's execution of Deng's foreign policy strategy began to change in the 1990s. China expanded and improved the quality of its interactions with the international community. These new directions in Chinese diplomacy began with efforts to break out of the international isolation following the Tiananmen incident; and these trends accelerated in the mid-1990s as China's economic integration with the global economy deepened, its global profile and influence grew, and Chinese perceptions of the international and regional security environments began to moderate. The changes in the *content* of China's foreign policy are best reflected in China's approach to its bilateral relations, its interactions with multilateral organizations, and its views on international security issues.

---

[40] For Chinese views on foreign policy issues see David Shambaugh, *Beautiful Imperialist*, Princeton, NJ: Princeton University Press, 1991. The foreign policymaking process in Deng's era is outlined in A. Doak Barnett, *The Making of Foreign Policy in China*, Washington, DC: John Hopkins School of Advanced International Studies, 1985.

Expanding Bilateral Relations

The foundation for these changes in China's diplomacy was a significant expansion of bilateral relations in the early 1990s. From 1988 to 1994, China normalized or established diplomatic relations with 18 countries, excluding the successor states of the Soviet Union. Moreover, much of this effort occurred in East Asia. China normalized relations with Laos, Vietnam, Malaysia, and Cambodia, while establishing ties with Singapore, South Korea, and Brunei. While the short-term goal was to consolidate China's position in the wake of the international isolation created by Tiananmen, the long-term effect was to solidify China's position in the Asia-Pacific region, especially the subregion of Southeast Asia. Today, the only countries that China does not currently recognize are those that have formal ties with Taiwan.

During the 1990s, China launched a diplomatic offensive to deepen the quality of ties with these 18 countries, especially those in the East Asian region. Dubbed "*da zhou bian wai jiao*" or "great regional diplomacy," Beijing moved to establish a range of high-quality partnerships (*huoban guanxi*) with nations in Asia as well as all over the world. These "partnerships" were meant to balance the perceived growth/expansion of U.S. alliances in Asia by qualitatively upgrading the economic, political, and in some cases military interactions between China and its neighboring countries.[41] China's use of the term "partnerships," which emphasizes "cooperation and coordination," is meant to contrast with the U.S. alliance relationships, which Beijing maintains reflect a "hegemonic Cold War mentality."

Engaging Multilateral Organizations

An increase in the quality of China's participation in multilateral and intergovernmental organizations has been one of the most important developments in the past five to eight years. Through the 1980s and early 1990s, China remained quite skeptical of such institutions, concerned that they might be used to punish or constrain China. Thomas Christensen wrote in 1996 that at that time China viewed regional forums as arenas to criticize, monitor, and constrain China.[42] Now, however, China sees them as venues for pursuing its economic interests, expanding its regional influence, addressing mutual security threats, and also checking U.S. regional influence. Importantly, China has founded, joined, or upgraded participation in fora in which the United States is not a member.

Starting in the second half of the 1990s, China started to engage with ASEAN and the Southeast Asian region in numerous multilateral fora. To ally fears about the impact of China's rise in both the security and economic realms, China increased the level and depth of its cooperation with ASEAN. China began to participate in the Asian Regional

---

[41] This notion of partnerships is outlined in Liu Huaqiu, "Writing a Bright and Colorful Chapter in Diplomatic Work," *Qiushi* [Truth], 1 November 2002. Also see Ruan Zongze, "Gouzhi xin shiji de dazhoubian waijiao [Setting Up the New Era's Great Regional Diplomacy]," *Liaowang* [Window], 17 September 2001, pp. 3-5.

[42] Thomas J. Christensen, "China's Realpolitik," *Foreign Affairs*, September/October 1996, pp. 37-52.

Forum in 1994, and it initiated the ASEAN 10 plus 3 and ASEAN plus 1 dialogues. In parallel, China has also deepened its participation in the Asia-Pacific Economic Cooperation forum, hosting the 9th Leader's Meeting in Shanghai in the fall of 2001. In Central Asia, China led the effort to establish one of the region's first multilateral organizations, known as the Shanghai Cooperation Organization (SCO). The SCO has focused on demilitarization of shared borders, counterterrorism activity, and regional trade. While China was clearly pursuing its own interests in establishing the SCO, what is interesting is that China turned to regional cooperation and not bilateral diplomacy.

Beyond Asia, Europe has also been a target for China's renewed engagement with the international community. In 1996, China was a founding member of the Asia-Europe Meeting, a dialogue with biennial summit meetings of heads of state and yearly meetings of ministers. In 1998, China and the EU initiated an annual political dialogue, which covers China-EU cooperation, trade, and human rights, all of which are designed to increase and deepen China's ties with the West.

Beijing's New Approach To Regional And International Security

China has become much more attentive to addressing a wide variety of traditional and nontraditional security challenges, demonstrating a new flexibility with its neighbors and an increased willingness to tackle transnational security issues. While Taiwan remains a key concern for mainland strategists and one still likely to lead to war, China has over time taken important new steps to recognize and defuse other emerging security concerns.

Throughout the 1990s, China has actively addressed numerous territorial disputes that have historically been the cause of substantial regional tension. Since 1991, China has settled disputes with Laos, Russia, Vietnam, Kazakhstan, Kyrgyzstan, and Tajikistan. In each and every settlement, China received 50 percent or less of the contested territory. In its long-standing dispute over the Pamir mountains that Tajikistan inherited from the Soviet Union, China received only 1,000 of the 28,000 sq km under dispute. While China and India have not been able to settle the dispute that led to war in 1962, the two sides have dramatically decreased tensions. Through two agreements, China and India have instituted significant troop reductions as well as confidence-building measures. Indeed, the "Line of Actual Control" in the Himalayas is increasingly viewed as a mutually acceptable border. China has also pursued similar troop reductions with Russia and the Central Asian states. China's long land border, the site of all of China's major wars, has never been more secure. China's acceptance of these boundaries is an important step forward. [43]

More generally, China has increased the quality of its participation in international security institutions. In the UN, China no longer abstains on critical votes in the UNSC, where it is a permanent member. In November 2002, China voted in support of UNSC Resolution 1441 calling for weapons inspections in Iraq. This was only the second time since China joined the UN in 1971 that it supported a Chapter Seven security council

---

[43] The authors are grateful to M. Taylor Fravel for providing these data and analysis.

resolution, which permits the use of force. China also importantly supported UNSC 1373, which calls for cooperation on tracking down financing for terrorists. Through the 1990s, while it generally did not block UN action, China abstained on similar votes, including during the first Gulf War. In addition to its increased participation in the UN, China approached NATO in the fall of 2002 about starting an annual dialogue on strategic perceptions. This proposal marked the first time that China had embarked upon such an effort with a U.S. security alliance, an effort that stands in stark contrast to China's traditionally critical approach.

Moreover, the past ten years have witnessed a significant evolution in China's involvement in international arms control and nonproliferation institutions. For much of the 1980s, China viewed arms control as the domain and responsibility of the United States and the Soviet Union. Nonproliferation was largely viewed as an effort by the United States to constrain China's regional and global influence and curtail its business activities in the Middle East and South Asia.

In the 1990s, much changed on this front. China joined most of the major multilateral arms control and nonproliferation accords, and it has also assumed numerous bilateral nonproliferation commitments. China joined the Treaty on the Nonproliferation of Nuclear Weapons, the Chemical Weapons Convention, and the Biological Weapons Convention; agreed to abide by the guidelines and parameters of the Missile Technology Control Regime, and joined a few multilateral supplier control regimes like the Zannger Committee and Australia Group. China notably also signed the Comprehensive Nuclear Test Ban Treaty in 1996.

Within the last 20 years, the geographic scope, technical content, and frequency of China's nuclear, missile, and chemical weapon-related exports have narrowed and diminished. Although China continues to provide some sensitive dual-use assistance to a few countries (such as Pakistan and Iran), China's nonproliferation practices have substantially improved. In the latter half of the 1990s, the Chinese government began to institutionalize its nonproliferation commitments by issuing export control regulations. This trend has accelerated in recent years, and a new round of regulations was issued in fall 2002. To be sure, China faces continued challenges implementing and enforcing these rules and regulations that, if not resolved, could call into question the leadership's political commitment to nonproliferation. An additional step has been the emergence during the past 20 years of a community of Chinese officials, scientists, military officers, and academics involved in nonproliferation policymaking. This community serves as an source of internal change in China and has played a critical role in sensitizing senior leaders about the importance of arms control and nonproliferation to China's overall foreign policy national security interests. In short, the trend lines of Chinese behavior on international arms control and nonproliferation issues continue to move in a direction consistent with international standards.

China's growing comfort and familiarity with arms control and nonproliferation issues were reflected in two episodes in the late 1990s. First, China led the UN effort in 1998 to oppose the nuclear tests in India and Pakistan, which resulted in UNSC Resolution 1172.

U.S. officials have repeatedly hailed China's leadership in condemning and responding to the tests. Second, China's efforts in the late 1990s to oppose U.S. support for ballistic missile defenses (BMD) demonstrated similar proactivity. Beijing was a central player in the international effort to oppose U.S. plans to withdraw from the ABM Treaty and deploy both national and theater missile defense capabilities. China sought to shape international public opinion. Drawing on its increased familiarity with multilateral forums, China led efforts in the UNSC and the Geneva-based Conference on Disarmament to oppose and constrain U.S. BMD plans. While China's anti-BMD diplomatic campaign ultimately failed because of Russian and European capitulation, this episode nonetheless represents a qualitative shift in Chinese diplomatic tactics.

Lastly, China's military diplomacy similarly reflects new thinking by Beijing about interacting with the international community. China has started to actively use its military-to-military ties with nations as a key tool with which to improve bilateral relations and bolster its regional profile. The case of Sino-South Korean relations is instructive in this regard. As China's economic ties with South Korea expanded in the 1990s, Beijing gradually started to upgrade Sino-South Korean military ties as a sign of an improving political relationship. This culminated in the unprecedented exchange of defense ministers in 2000. Moreover, China in 2001 conducted the first peacetime combined military exercise with other nations outside China's borders. This counterterrorism exercise with the military forces of Kyrgyzstan was unprecedented in China's history and clearly indicates some innovative thinking in China about the use of military diplomacy as a tool to bolster its regional security relations.[44]

New Approach To Taiwan: New Maturity Or Wishful Thinking?

Beijing's recent approach to the Taiwan issue, its greatest security challenge and most controversial "foreign" policy issue, also curiously reflected a growing confidence in 2002 and 2003. From the mid-1990s to the middle of 2000, China's strategy in addressing cross-strait relations and U.S. ties with Taiwan represented the apex of a conservative, insecure, and reactive foreign policy. Beijing was so nervous about creeping independence that it viewed many of its foreign policy decisions (such as critical bilateral relationships) through the prism the Taiwan issue.[45] Beijing's boisterous and threat-oriented policies were focused far more on coercion and preventing independence than encouraging Taiwan to reunify. During that time period, Chinese officials protested each and every little improvement in U.S.-Taiwan military ties and increasingly emphasized that the Taiwan issue was a source of conflict in U.S.-China relations. This approach was resoundingly counterproductive for China. In 1995 and 1996, China conducted missile tests off Taiwan's coastline after efforts by Taiwan's president to expand the island's international space. Instead of bringing Taiwan to heel and deterring the United States, these tests compelled Washington to dispatch two carriers to the Strait and then President Lee Teng-hui actually gained votes in the 1996

---

[44] *China's National Defense in 2002*, Beijing, China: Information Office of the State Council, 2003, pp. 70-72.

[45] Evan A. Feigenbaum, "China's Challenge to Pax Americana," *Washington Quarterly*, Summer 2001, pp. 31-43.

election. China's military exercises and bellicose language also damaged China's image in the region, particularly among Southeast Asian nations. A similar mistake happened four years later. Beijing's 2000 White Paper on Taiwan noted that Taiwan's indefinite delay in restarting cross-strait negotiations would be tantamount to a declaration of independence and could inevitably result in China's use of force. China, in effect, had set up a timetable for reunification. Several months later Taiwan elected for the first time a nominally pro-independence president.

In recent years Beijing's pervasive insecurity and its coercive policies on the Taiwan issue were replaced fro a time with a confidence born of booming cross-strait economic interactions, a modernizing military, and perceived favorable political trends in Taiwan. The 2000 timetable for reunification was abandoned. Chinese leaders no longer protest each and every little up-tick in U.S.-Taiwan military ties. Chinese policymakers recognized the failure of their past approach and replaced it with one that sought to seduce Taiwan with economic opportunities while gradually sharpening its coercive tools.[46] Patience and confidence, for a time, replaced insecurity on the Taiwan issue. Though, given the extreme volatility of this issue in Chinese internal politics, this approach did not last long. In late 2003, in the lead up to Taiwan's presidential election, Chen Shui-bian inflamed Beijing's insecurities through words and actions about his ultimate quest for independence. This behavior, followed by Chen's reelection in 2004, led Beijing to once again embrace its hardnosed and inflexible approach to restarting cross-Strait dialogue.

CHANGING CHARACTER AND EXECUTION OF CHINESE FOREIGN POLICY

The changing content of China's diplomacy is matched by gradual shifts in the way that Beijing internally formulates and then externally articulates its foreign policies. Both the leaders and processes of foreign policy decisionmaking have become more sophisticated. China's senior policymakers (especially in the foreign and trade ministries) are more cosmopolitan than any preceding generation. Most have traveled extensively in the region and in other parts of the world. In the 1990s, China's foreign policy decisionmaking processes continued with past trends by becoming more institutionalized and routinized. The importance of these trends is that ultimately they enhance the role of bureaucratic players over individual leaders. A number of bureaucratic changes were initiated to bolster interagency coordination. The November 2000 formation of a National Security Leading Small Group to handle crisis management is one such example. [47]

A key component of China's new foreign policy decisionmaking is the increasing diversification of foreign policy analysis inside and outside of government. Within the Foreign Ministry, a newly invigorated Policy Planning Department plays a prominent role in developing policy options as an internal think tank. On certain issues, the Chinese government has hired outside specialists with functional or regional expertise to consult

---

[46] See the later section on new directions in Chinese military modernization.

[47] Some of these trends on institutionalization are also addressed in Lampton, ed., "The Making of Chinese Foreign and Security Policy," op. cit.

on ongoing policy debates. Many of China's scholars regularly travel outside of China and interact with international experts in their field. These scholars and analysts have emerged as an important channel to sensitize leaders to international trends and to present informed and creative policy options to leaders.[48]

Another important dynamic has been the increase in public debates on global trends and, notably, China's responses to them. The latter types of public discussions were unheard of ten years ago. This suggests that in a broad sense public opinion in China is beginning to have more and more influence on policymaker's decisions. This is particularly true in the current political climate in which the CCP is straining to prove its continued relevance and credibility.

Perhaps one of the newest and starkest changes in Chinese foreign policy in the past decade has been China's dedicated and consistent effort to publicize and promote its foreign policy views. In past decades, Chinese policies, opinions, and perspectives were relegated to obscure *Xinhua* and *People's Daily* news reports, small Foreign Ministry pamphlets, and arcane academic journals. While sinologists regularly ferreted out these materials, Chinese views were not widely articulated or understood beyond a small community of international China watchers. Beijing has substantially improved its ability to market and sell its world views and foreign policies in an effort to bolster its international image. This development represents a novel and important pillar of China's new diplomacy. In May 2000, the Foreign Ministry opened a new media center that provides regular press briefings at least twice a week. Beijing also promotes its views through the publication of numerous "white papers" and a deft exploitation of the Internet. The Ministry of Foreign Affairs (MFA) web site (www.fmprc.gov.cn) is a trove of useful data on past and present foreign policy. Each division in the MFA has a separate web page that describes China's official position on regional and functional issues--topics previously seldom addressed in publications and statements. While many of these statements are anodyne and boilerplate, they provide one stop shopping on China's official foreign policy.

CHINA IN A POST-9/11 WORLD: EMERGENCE OF INNOVATIVE FOREIGN POLICY THINKING

The changes in the content, character, and execution of China's foreign policy noted above have been far more evolutionary than revolutionary. Most have gradually emerged over the past five to ten years as China sought to promote economic development and internal stability, to break out of the Tiananmen isolation, to hinder Taiwan's efforts to increase its international profile, to preserve its regional influence, and to balance the unexpected growth of U.S. influence in Asia.

Yet, in the past three years and especially after 9/11 and the corresponding improvement in U.S.-China relations, some very innovative and revolutionary thinking about Chinese diplomacy has emerged in both academic and policymaking circles. The writings and

---

[48] Bonnie Glaser and Phillip C. Saunders, "Chinese Civilian Foreign Policy Research Institutes: Evolving Roles and Increasing Influence," *The China Quarterly*, September 2002, pp. 597-616.

statements of Chinese policymakers and scholars have begun to reflect a critical shift in China's views of the structure of the international system and, most important, the role China seeks to play in international affairs. Some of this new thinking interestingly contrasts with China's previously articulated New Security Concept (NSC), which is China's answer to U.S. concepts of global order and "Cold War thinking."[49] These trends at least suggest the beginning of a potentially significant transformation of China's world view and its diplomacy. This subsection identifies five areas of new thinking on international affairs in China.

First, articles in major newspapers (such as *People's Daily* and *Global Times*) and journals have specifically advocated discarding China's long-held victim mentality and the persistent emphasis on "the century of shame and humiliation" as the main perceptual lens through which Chinese view their place in world affairs. These writings suggest a major shift in China's "national role concept." Influential Chinese analysts have begun to promote China's adoption of a "great power mentality" (*daguo xintai*). This emerging notion seeks to replace China's victim mentality with a confidence born of two decades of impressive economic growth and development, and Beijing's growing influence in global economic and security affairs.[50]

A second major aspect of this new thinking is a grudging acceptance that the world is unipolar and that U.S. preponderant power will persist for years if not decades in the future. While Chinese leaders publicly tout multipolarization as the trend of the times, Chinese analysts of late privately acknowledge that China will not challenge U.S. global dominance in the future. Wang Jisi, a noted Chinese foreign policy expert, in a recent publication distinguishes between a hegemonic power and hegemonic behavior. China can accept the former but not the latter. Wang argues that "peace and development" can still flourish in a unipolar world but that it will likely be an unjust peace that does not serve all of China's interests--such as allowing it an unfettered ability to coerce Taiwan.

Third, Chinese strategists increasingly argue that China needs to focus more on great power relations (*da guo guanxi*) as a priority in its foreign relations. Interactions with neighboring nations and developing countries are seen by many, though not all, as secondary and tertiary priorities for China. Jiang Zemin outlined such a prioritization for China's foreign relations in his work report to the 16th Party Congress in November 2002. Chinese scholars and strategists argue that China's economic and strategic interests are far closer to those of the major powers, especially those in Asia such as South Korea and Japan. Many Chinese assert that counterterrorism cooperation in the wake of 9/11, Operation Enduring Freedom, and Operation Iraqi Freedom have made "great power relations" a defining feature of current global politics.[51]

---

[49] China's NSC promotes multilateralism and bilateral "partnerships " as an alternative to U.S. reliance on regional alliances. For the substance of the NSC, see Roy, op. cit.

[50] Jin Xide, "Zhongguo xuyao daguo xintai [China Needs a Great Power Mentality]," *Huanqiu shibao* [Global Times], 12 September 2002, p. 4; Ye Zicheng and Li Ying, "Zhongguo suoyi bixu jian daguo waijiao xintai [China Therefore Continues to Establish a Great Power Foreign Policy Mentality]," *Huanqiu shibao*, 20 July 2001.

[51] Gu Dexin, "Mei-Yi Zhanzheng yu Zhongguo guojia anquan [U.S.-Iraq War and China's National Security]," *Xiandai guoji guanxi*, No. 4, 2003, pp. 2-22.

Fourth, Chinese analysts openly argue that China, as a rising power, needs to pay attention to not only its rights but also its responsibilities as a great power. As Beijing's power and influence increases, Chinese analysts argue that more nations will call upon China to shoulder its global responsibilities. They conclude that the demands on China to act in ways more consistent with international norms will grow.[52] This idea frequently manifests itself in the growing and frequent Chinese use of the phrase "shared global responsibilities" to describe modern interactions among major powers.

A final key element of this new thinking is an explicit recognition that--as a result of many of the preceding conclusions--China needs to play a more active and constructive role in world affairs. This conclusion flies in the face of Chinese conventional wisdom on foreign affairs of not taking risks and not taking the lead (*bu dang tou*). Chinese analysts are now arguing that China's economic and political interests are so intertwined with the international system that Beijing can protect and promote them only by beginning to play a role in shaping the international system. Chinese analysts make this somewhat provocative argument by safely quoting Deng Xiaoping's aphorism "*you suo zuo wei*" which calls for "getting some things done." In doing so they seek to deemphasize the other oft quoted Dengism "*tao guang yang hui*" or "hiding our capabilities and biding our time." The most forward leaning analysts even argue that China needs to move beyond Deng Xiaoping's 28-character slogan on foreign policy (which stresses moderation) to a new set of more creative and proactive "guidelines" for its foreign policy.[53]

There are preliminary indications that some of this new thinking has begun to manifest in Chinese policy decisions. In broad terms, China has been paying much more attention to nontraditional security issues such as counternarcotics, nonproliferation, and counterterrorism. Previously, these were viewed as the purview of developed nations that had the time and resources to devote to them. China's growing attention to environmental and health crises suggests a further sensitization to transnational issues as sources of instability for China, and thus a set of issues that demand attention.

In terms of specific policy decisions, Beijing has taken a far more active role on the North Korea nuclear issue than in past years. As noted above, China used coercive means, including temporary freezes on oil transfers, to prod the North to participate in tripartite talks with the United States and China. China has assumed a leadership role in the Shanghai Cooperation Organization. Not only did it help form the organization but the secretariat is now based in Beijing. Perhaps most interesting, under the rubric of anti-terrorism cooperation in the SCO, China in 2002 conducted its *first ever* peacetime military exercise with another country (Kyrgyzstan) and in 2004 conducted maritime exercises with France and Great Britain. Earlier this year, China sent its first envoy to the Middle East to express China's interests in helping to resolve the Israel-Palestine problem. More recently, Chinese President Hu Jintao agreed to attend a meeting of the G-8 as a dialogue member. For many past years China declined such invitations by arguing

---

[52] Wang Jisi, "Xin xingshi de zhuyao tedian he Zhongguo de waijiao [The Main Characteristics of the New Situation and Chinese Diplomacy]," *Xiandai guoji guanxi*, No. 4, 2003, pp. 1-3.

[53] Dong Fangxiao, "Zhibian qiubian [Knowing and Seeking Change]," *Xiandai guoji guanxi*, No. 4, 2003, pp. 26-28.

that China viewed the G-8 as a "club of rich nations" operating outside the framework of the UNSC.

CONCLUSION

The evolution of Chinese foreign policy from Deng's somewhat limited and passive approach represents one of the most important transformations for China in the past decade. The content, character, and execution of foreign policy have morphed in ways that have augmented the quality of China's interaction with the international community, raised China's global profile, and broadened the possibilities of international cooperation.

Yet, the scope, speed, and longevity of these changes are an open question since they are emerging in a conservative context. As Jonathan Spence eloquently pointed out in his 1969 tome *To Change China*, Confucian culture has effectively resisted change from external influences for hundreds of years. Mao's mixing of Communist-Leninist organizational principles with Confucian culture has resulted in a particularly truculent social and political context for change and transformation. The constraints on rapid transformation of Chinese foreign policy are significant and should not be underestimated.

Beijing's top and enduring priority, for example, is economic development and internal stability. The extent to which foreign policy decisions facilitate that paramount aim will enable (or constrain) the further evolution in Chinese diplomacy. Furthermore, the persistence of an essentially Leninist political system creates disincentives for the type of innovative and creative thinking that serves as the genesis for enduring changes in perceptions and policies. Foreign policy debates in China are particularly sensitive to these dynamics. The growing demand for consensus in Beijing will further limit the degree of innovation in foreign policy decisionmaking. Moreover, China lacks soft power in international relations. What principles does China stand for and, more important, why should other nations listen to Beijing or follow its policies? These are questions that senior officials in China will need to address.

The ever-shifting context of U.S.-China relations will continue to wield a strong influence on Chinese perceptions of the international security environment and China's policy responses to global affairs. The surprising improvement in Beijing's ties with Washington after 9/11 has produced much greater optimism in Beijing about the decline of "contradictions" in global affairs and has seemingly boosted China's willingness to cooperate on a host of transnational security challenges like terrorism and proliferation. Given the persistent and substantial preoccupation by Chinese strategists on U.S. foreign and security policies, the recent up-tick in U.S.-China relations bodes well for China's continuing evolution toward becoming a more cooperative member of the international community. Though a downturn in U.S.-China relations could precipitate a retrenchment in some of the recent and progressive trends in Chinese thinking about foreign affairs.

Continued transformation in Chinese thinking about its role in the world and its foreign policies will be gradual. If the "new thinking" in China on foreign affairs is any indication, China will gradually become a potent force in shaping international debates and institutions. U.S. and international policymakers should welcome such a development but also treat it with equal prudence. The possibilities for eliciting cooperation from China may increase as U.S., European, and Chinese interests increasingly overlap. At the same time, China will become better at manipulating international organizations and bilateral relationships in ways conducive to achieving its foreign policy interests. The potential for partnership on pressing security and economic issues will grow, but--on issues of discord or disagreement--China will be better equipped to confront and challenge the interests, preferences, and policies of the prevailing regional or global powers. These dueling possibilities present the international community with a complex set of nested challenges and opportunities that will shape an evolving international security landscape in the years to come.

V. CHANGES IN CHINESE MILITARY MODERNIZATION POLICIES

CHANGING PLA VIEWS OF THE INTERNATIONAL SECURITY ENVIRONMENT

The changes in the international security environment described above have had a profound impact on the threat perceptions of the Chinese military and have significantly shaped the trajectory of PLA modernization, rapidly accelerating a program of equipment upgrades and doctrinal revision that had heretofore been relatively gradual. In the early to mid-1980s, the PLA obeyed Deng Xiaoping's mantra that "peace and development" were the trend of the time and acquiesced to almost a decade of defense budgets that declined in real terms. After the civilian leadership concluded in 1985 that major war between the superpowers was unlikely, the writings of PLA strategists about the nature of the international security environment were relatively unfocused, cautiously appraising trends at the end of the Cold War and making tentative inquiries into new areas like the security issues related to the South China Sea. Both the civilian and military systems during this period were focused on the economy, viewing the international system as a plentiful source of technology, capital, and know-how for market growth.

Yet the international opprobrium generated by the massacre of civilians in Tiananmen Square, as well as the subsequent embargo against military goods, served as a harsh reminder to the PLA that the outside world could still negatively affect China's national interests. The potency of these external dangers was reinforced by the U.S. victory in the first Gulf War, in which Chinese-vintage weaponry was ruthlessly annihilated by coalition forces testing prototypes of systems related to the revolution in military affairs. More important, the changing political strategy of Taiwan President Lee Teng-hui in the early 1990s, particularly his expressed desire to expand Taiwan's international relationships, raised new alarms among PLA strategists. This escalating tension in cross-strait relations was dramatically manifest in the 1995-1996 missile exercise crisis, though the decision of the United States to send aircraft carrier battle groups to the areas surrounding Taiwan arguably had a more profound impact, significantly raising the stakes for Beijing and the PLA. From that point forward, the Taiwan contingency, including the possibility of U.S. military intervention, became the core planning justification for PLA procurement, doctrinal revision, training, education, and command, control, communications, computers, and intelligence (C4I) modernization.

Since 1996, continuing negative trends across the Strait have further alarmed the Chinese military and civilian leadership. Among the most important trends are a perception of further moves by Taiwan toward de facto independence since 1996, the failure of the PRC's coercive political strategy to prevent this erosion of the "status quo," and the perceived expansion of U.S.-Taiwan military-to-military relations. At the same time, Sino-U.S. relations experienced a series of crises, beginning with the bombing of the Chinese Embassy in Belgrade in April 1999, which unleashed a torrent of nationalist emotion and calls for greater attention to improving military capabilities. The subsequent debate over the international security environment directly challenged Deng's earlier dicta. While "peace and development" were retained as the theme of the era, the phrase was thereafter followed by ominous statements about unnamed negative trends in international stability. The perceived threat from U.S. "hegemonism" became explicit after the EP-3A collision and hostage crisis in April 2001, and PLA strategist writings since then have clearly identified the United States as a threat to Chinese national interests, particularly the goal of achieving "reunification" with Taiwan.

THE RELATIONSHIP BETWEEN PERCEPTIONS AND MILITARY MODERNIZATION

In parallel to this shift in perceptions, PLA modernization has moved from a relatively low national priority to a core element of national policy. In the early 1990s, when PLA strategists began to worry about Taiwan, China initially looked to foreign suppliers of military equipment, particularly Russia, to fill niche requirements for a Taiwan contingency quickly. These purchases of small numbers of high-quality equipment were rightly interpreted by outside observers as a scathing indictment of the failures of the indigenous defense-industrial base to produce the necessary equipment in a timely manner. Early acquisitions included Su-27 fighter aircraft, which could facilitate over-water air superiority and were a credible counter to the advanced fighter aircraft (Mirage 2000, F-16) purchased by Taiwan; Kilo-class submarines, which could be used to blockade Taiwanese ports and, along with the Sovremenny-class destroyers and its advanced ship-to-ship cruise missile (SS-N-22 SUNBURN), prosecute an access denial strategy against the United States Navy; SA-10/15/20 surface-to-air missiles (SAMs), intended to enhance Chinese air superiority over the Strait and defend the mainland against offensive air operations by the United States and/or Taiwan; and the A-50 MAINSTAY system for battle space management of Chinese air forces, similar to the U.S. Airborne Warning and Control System or Israeli Phalcon. More recent purchases include the Su-30MKK, which replaces the A-5 fighter as China's premier air-to-ground attack platform.

This early period of modernization also witnessed some progress by the indigenous defense industrial base. Perhaps the greatest success has occurred in ballistic missiles, particularly short-range ballistic missiles and land-attack cruise missiles aimed at Taiwan as well as longer-range missiles for strategic forces, which are discussed in more detail in the next subsection. Dramatic successes have also been achieved in C4I modernization, thanks to the phenomenal rise of the Chinese IT sector, including telecommunications equipment manufacturing.[54] Niche successes have also been achieved in the shipbuilding sector, thanks again to strong development of the civilian shipbuilding sector, though progress in aviation and ordnance has been more platform-specific. More important, the quality and quantity of defense-industrial output has clearly accelerated since 1999, as the heightened sense of urgency fostered by the Belgrade bombing led to civilian leadership support for significant increases in the official defense budget.

---

[54] James Mulvenon, "The Digital Triangle," in Edward L. Hughes and Kent H. Butts, eds., *Economics and National Security: The Case of China*, Carlisle Barracks, PA: U.S. Army War College Center for Strategic Leadership, 2001.

Additional, equally important advances have been made in "softer" aspects of military modernization, including education and training. It is difficult to link them directly to changes in the international security environment, however, since many of these changes in structure and personnel started more than 25 years ago. Following the destructive period of the Cultural Revolution, the PLA education system has been largely reconstituted, consolidated, and modernized, with greater emphasis on modern warfare, science and technology, foreign military studies, and nonmilitary topics.[55] The 1990s witnessed the rise of a genuine noncommissioned officer corps, providing greater institutional memory within combat units and reducing conscription demands.[56] A joint logistics system has been implemented at the military region level, initially permitting service units to use each other's medical and petroleum, oil, and lubricants facilities.[57] Finally, the PLA has implemented a higher-tempo training schedule, involving exercises that are larger in scale and longer in duration than previous efforts and involving the coordination of larger military units, participation of units from different military regions, and joint operations with naval, air, and ground forces.[58]

STRATEGIC FORCES CASE STUDY

A possible case study of PLA responses to changes in the international security environment is China's current program of strategic nuclear modernization. China is one of a handful of nuclear weapon states that is engaged in a comprehensive nuclear force upgrade. Far from being a piecemeal attempt at improving certain specific platforms, this program is oriented toward upgrading the entire panoply of Chinese strategic nuclear assets: the number, quality, and type of nuclear warheads and delivery systems; the command and control system; the supporting infrastructure and procedural systems; and the doctrinal basis of nuclear strategy.[59] The future Chinese nuclear force will likely

---

[55] Thomas Bickford, "Professional Military Education in the Chinese People's Liberation Army: A Preliminary Assessment of Problems and Prospects," in James C. Mulvenon and Andrew N.D. Yang, eds., *A Poverty of Riches: New Challenges and Opportunities in PLA Research*, Santa Monica, CA: The RAND Corporation, CF-189-NSRD, 2003.

[56] Dennis Blasko, "People's War Lives On: Chinese Military Logistics in the War Zone" (unpublished paper.)

[57] See Lonnie Henley, "PLA Logistics and Doctrine Reform, 1999-2009," in Susan Puska, ed., *People's Liberation Army After Next*, Carlisle Barracks, PA: U.S. Army War College Strategic Studies Institute, 2000, pp. 55-78.

[58] Dennis Blasko, Philip Klapakis , and John F. Corbett, Jr., "Training Tomorrow's PLA: A Mixed Bag of Tricks," *China Quarterly*, June 1996.

[59] Historically, the Chinese nuclear force was marked by a relatively small number of warheads; technically and numerically limited delivery vehicles; an overwhelming reliance on land-based systems; persistent concerns over the arsenal's survivability, reliability, and penetrability; and a limited program of research, development, and testing. China's current nuclear weapons arsenal totals about 400 devices, 300 of which consist of warheads and gravity bombs for use on its strategic "triad" of land-based ballistic missiles, bomber and attack aircraft, and one nuclear-powered ballistic missile submarine (SSBN). Viewed as an organic whole, the Chinese nuclear force structure defies simple categorization as either a limited or minimal deterrent. Instead, the multifaceted force is made up of strategic, theater, and tactical systems of varying range, accuracy, and yield. The small ICBM force, anchored by the DF-5 family of missiles, appears to be a second-strike minimal deterrence force. The theater systems are unlikely to be used in a second-strike, minimal deterrent role following a preemptive strike. Instead, theater systems look like offensive systems meant to strike U.S. forces and bases in Asia to degrade conventional capability. The

possess a number of new characteristics, including mobility, solid fuel, improved C4I, greater accuracy, higher numbers of reentry vehicles, and even a more conventional orientation in warheads.

In these respects, Beijing's strategic forces modernization effort is an exception to the general international trend toward the reduction of the utility of nuclear weapons in world politics. Yet it is important to note that China's nuclear modernization effort has been ongoing for 30 years, predating both Star Wars and the more recent efforts to develop a national missile defense system. For example, China's next-generation intercontinental ballistic missile (ICBM)--the solid-fueled, road-mobile DF-31--was initiated in 1969. For the last 30-plus years, technology has been the primary driver of doctrine and deployment, though more as a constraint than a facilitator.[60] Only in the past decade has the missile modernization effort found traction and accelerated.

There are a number of impetuses behind the modernization of the Chinese nuclear force structure, none of which involve *recent* changes in the international security environment. Indeed, China's nuclear forces are much more affected by long-term strategic shifts, not two- to three-year tactical shifts, primarily because of the long lead times of these platforms. The first is the predictable process of replacing aging weapons systems with more modern counterparts. We must entertain the definite possibility that the new generation of missiles is meant only to replace the aging veterans of the fleet, particularly the DF-4 and DF-5. If the Chinese eventually exchange the road-mobile, solid-fueled DF-31s and DF-41s for these liquid-fueled, silo- and cave-based missiles on a one-to-one basis, or even two-to-one basis, then the net result is *ceteris paribus* an increase in the credibility of China's previously suspect minimal deterrent, not necessarily a fundamental shift to an offensive posture. Moreover, as the significant delays in the initial operational capability of past systems and the inaccurate estimates of DF-31/DF-41/DF-25 deployments in Lewis and Hua's seminal 1992 article attest, we should not be overly optimistic about the production timelines or output estimates offered by the Chinese for the rollout of the next generation of missiles, but should instead maintain a sober view of the impressive but sometimes erratic production cycles in the Chinese missile system.[61]

The second important factor behind the modernization of China's strategic forces is the shifting postures of traditional nuclear powers, such as Russia and the United States, and emerging nuclear powers in Asia, particularly India. Historically, the level and deployment pattern of China's nuclear forces were first oriented to deal with a Soviet invasion from the north, and then altered in the 1980s and 1990s to address growing concerns about deterring the United States and targeting in-theater forces in Japan, Guam, and Korea, as well as countervalue targets in the continental United States. More

---

short-range, ballistic missile forces, which are also nuclear capable, further confuse the situation by serving a variety of conventional war-fighting and nuclear war-fighting roles.

[60] John Wilson Lewis and Xue Litai, *China's Strategic Seapower: The Politics of Force Modernization in the Nuclear Age*, Stanford: Stanford University Press, 1994; and John Wilson Lewis and Xue Litai, *China Builds the Bomb*, Stanford, CA: Stanford University Press, 1988.

[61] John Wilson Lewis and Xue Litai, "China's Ballistic Missile Programs: Technologies, Strategies, Goals," *International Security*, Vol. 17, No. 2, Fall 1992.

recently, Chinese nuclear planners have been forced to confront the possibility of a new southwestern "front" opening up with India, demanding a possible increase in projected force levels and unexpected changes in deployment patterns.

A third and perhaps critical driver behind China's strategic modernization is a rising concern about the credibility of its nuclear deterrent, which the nation has sought to remedy by improving the readiness, survivability, and reliability of the force. While these concerns have existed for decades, they have become more acute in the past ten years, particularly with the renewed U.S. interest in the deployment of theater and national missile defenses. While missile defenses are not responsible for Chinese strategic modernization, ongoing research and development as well as planned initial deployments in 2004 will likely accelerate China's efforts and push Beijing to spend more money on relatively cheap antimissile defense countermeasures and decoys. Moreover, leaks from the most recent Nuclear Posture Review, particularly the revelation about targeting of China in the single integrated operation plan, raise further concerns among Chinese strategists about the instability of a possible preemptive U.S. attack against the PRC force, with missile defenses able to capture any stragglers.

Thanks to the imminent deployment of the DF-31, the PRC is therefore nearing an historic convergence between doctrine and capability, allowing it to increasingly achieve a degree of *credible minimal deterrence* vis-à-vis the continental United States--a convergence of its doctrine and capability that it has not confidently possessed since the weaponization of China's nuclear program in the mid-1960s. Paradoxically, this deployment would increase deterrence stability between China and other nuclear powers and allow China to maintain a no-first-use principle by reducing the likelihood that the PRC's force could be destroyed in an all-out preemptive attack. Yet Chinese nuclear strategists are deeply worried that "no first use" is a liability as long as PRC nuclear forces remain in silos, since U.S. conventional forces can destroy fixed targets with precision-guided munitions. The corresponding failure of the same forces to destroy mobile targets no doubt reinforced the perceived desirability of modern, road-mobile nuclear forces.

At the same time, as long as the numbers of the force stay beneath a certain level, increases in accuracy and multiple warheads do not pose a threat to American and Russian overwhelming nuclear superiority, though the smaller French and British arsenals may face greater challenges as Chinese nuclear forces grow in number. American strategic nuclear forces still number around 8,000 deployed on 575 ICBMs, 102 strategic bombers, and 17 Nuclear Ballistic Missile Submarines (SSBNs). Indeed, a single *Trident* SSBN, carries more missiles (24) than the entire Chinese ICBM inventory.

The troubling countertrend involves the introduction of theater and national missile defenses into the equation, dramatically complicating China's strategic environment. Whereas China previously faced a world marked by the threat of an arms race in offensive nuclear weapons, the post-BMD world will be marked by the unpredictable interactions of races for both offensive and defensive strategic weapons and for countermeasures/decoys. In this environment, China would be acting rationally if it accelerated the desultory pace of its missile modernization, spending more money on relatively cheap countermeasures and decoys. In order to develop smaller warheads for penetrating missile defenses, it would be acting in its self-interest by opting out of the Comprehensive Nuclear Test Ban Treaty and resuming testing. Finally, China might even seek to foil missile defenses by proliferating its countermeasures technology to other emerging nuclear states.

CONCLUSION

To summarize, this section argues that changes in the international security environment have had a profound impact on the threat perceptions of the PLA and its civilian masters, creating bureaucratic and political support for increased defense spending and accelerated military modernization. Of these, two of the most important perceived changes were the rise of dominant U.S. military power--as evidenced in Gulf Wars I & II, Kosovo, Afghanistan, and Iraq--combined with the evident desire on the part of the sole remaining superpower to use that military power to pursue a global unilateral agenda, including the prevention of Chinese reunification with Taiwan. As a result of these trends, PLA modernization was elevated from a relatively low priority to a core element of national policy. Niche capabilities were filled with high-tech acquisitions from Russian defense industries and labs, while the PLA underwent massive internal reform in almost every key area, including education, training, organization, and doctrine. More recently, two decades of wrenching change in the Chinese defense industries have begun to bear fruit, resulting in significant increases in the quality and quantity of production in aviation, shipbuilding, ordnance, and command, control, communications, computers, intelligence, surveillance, and reconnaissance (C4ISR).

At the same time, the case study examination of Chinese strategic forces modernization reveals a much more tenuous linkage with short-term changes in the international security environment. Instead, technological determinist impulses, longer-term shifts in relations with declared nuclear powers, and longstanding concerns about the lack of credibility of China's nuclear deterrent appear to be far more compelling rationales for the current course and trajectory of Beijing's force posture changes.

Looking to the future, the pace and robustness of PLA modernization are far from certain, given the monumental challenges faced by the fourth generation leadership in fostering high rates of economic growth, preventing a banking crisis, maintaining social stability, and staving off massive environmental disaster, to name a few. Yet, so far the leadership has seemed willing to provide the PLA with annual double-digit budget increases, despite the increasing budget deficits and other warning signs, because of the strategic imperative of achieving a capability to successfully coerce Taiwan into reunifying while deterring U.S. military intervention. As a result, PLA modernization will likely be sustained at current levels, barring any significant downturn in state capacity. Particularly salient indicators of this continuing commitment will be found in the level of resources provided for expensive, high-tech acquisitions from Russia and investment in the indigenous defense-industrial sector.

VI. CONCLUSION: CHINA, EUROPE, AND THE UNITED STATES

The United States exerts a powerful influence on China's environment, but China is determined to gain strategic space as its capabilities improve. One way of doing so is to capitalize on its standing in East Asia, its huge economic capacity, and the present-day shadow of its future power in order to build relationships with other actors. Europe is one such actor, perhaps as important as any. While Europe and the United States have largely common aims regarding China, the Chinese may view Europe as a potential counterweight to the United States, especially as EU-level decisionmaking matures and European involvement in East Asia expands. In turn, because of China's regional clout and global potential, Europeans will want their own relationship with China, rather than merely following America's lead. The recent EU debate about lifting the arms export embargo on China may be a manifestation of both of these trends. Chinese leaders have lobbied their EU counterparts that the embargo is anachronistic at the very time that EU policymakers are trying to forge their own, distinct economic and geopolitical ties with China.

Of course, the respective positions of the United States and Europe in East Asia are profoundly asymmetric. For the United States, a prominent security role in East Asia is a pillar of its global standing and central to its alliance commitments. Accordingly, it has a more or less clear regional strategy, and it policies shape the choices of countries, large and small, throughout the region. In contrast, East Asia does not figure importantly in the outlooks of Europe and its nations. European policies toward the region lack coherence and purpose, and they have little effect on East Asian affairs. Even European-Japanese relations have never developed as one might have expected for two of the world's three leading economies.

If there is an exception to this pattern of the European approach to Asia, it could be China. Several European countries have built up their own relationships with China in recent decades, and the EU's nascent foreign and security policy has devoted more attention to formulating policies toward China than toward any other non-European nation (except for the United States, of course). Meanwhile, the United States has begun to face the consequences of China's rising regional economic, diplomatic, and military importance. No longer can the United States--supported by such privileged allies as Japan, Korea, and Australia--manage the region without regard for Chinese equities and reactions.

This suggests the possibility of a triangle--if a rather oddly shaped one--among China, Europe, and America, with a disquieting potential if translated into strategic maneuvering by each between the other two. Presently, neither the United States nor the EU and its member states, including France, explicitly or implicitly base their relations with China on triangular calculations. Rather, the two follow parallel interests vis-à-vis China: utilizing its productive capacities, accessing its potentially vast market, committing it to international trade rules, and shaping its policies on nonproliferation, human rights, and environmental security. Yet two factors make a triangular game possible.

First, Chinese leaders are predisposed by their ancient strategic culture to seek leverage through foreign relationships. Even during the Cold War, Europe was seen by China, naively as it turned out, as a possible battleground for influence to reduce superpower dominance. More recently, and less naively, China has come to regard Europe as critical to achieving a multipolar alternative to a U.S.-centric unipolar world. The Chinese are well aware that Europeans are not entirely comfortable with their unequal relationship with the United States, especially after a decade of superior U.S. economic growth and, lately, perceived heavy-handed American policies. The Chinese may feel that Europeans could be drawn into cooperation aimed at balancing and constraining the United States.

Second, it is presently the United States that sets the agenda and shapes the environment of China. Although the Chinese do not admit this, neither can they be content with it. While America's exports to China remain lackluster (like Europe's), the enormous Chinese trade surplus with the United States provides the net importer, not the exporter, with strategic leverage. Throughout East Asia, the web of U.S.-based alliances and market positions enjoyed by American firms, especially in high-technology, ensures that America is China's main, often only, strategic interlocutor. These trends are mutually reinforcing. For the United States, having leverage on Asian strategic issues serves its economic and commercial interests; in turn, the magnitude of those interests ensures continued U.S. domestic support for a robust regional role.

For Europeans, the inverse is true: Participation in East-Asian politics has a relatively high cost of entry and often meets with American resistance, especially when important U.S. security and economic interests are at stake. While realism dictates deep U.S. economic and strategic involvement in the region, the same sort of realism may suggest to Europeans that they should sit on the sidelines, letting the United States shoulder the burdens and risks, or being poised to exploit the difficulties of America's responsibilities.

Nowhere is this as evident as in the case of China. While not adversaries, China and the United States are strategic and political competitors in the region. Yet, their economic symbiosis grows stronger with every year that passes. Of course, economic relations are also increasing between China and Europe. However, Europe does not possess the requisite military reach or supranational policymaking capacity to be a powerful and purposeful actor in East Asian strategic politics, vis-à-vis either China or the United States. As long as Europe remains on the margin of East Asian power politics, neither China nor the United States can use its European relationship to strengthen its hand toward the other.

Still, a triangular logic may be creeping into relations among China, the United States, and Europe. There is, after all, little reward for Europeans to align themselves with United States policies toward China, especially given the constant vacillations. For its part, the United States has an interest in keeping control of the relationship with China by acting largely alone or by enlisting "partners"--followers, really--in coalitions that support its aims. The temptation for triangular games is only natural where commercial competition is concerned, even under WTO rules. Asia in general and China in particular are emerging as key potential markets for high-technology goods and services--from civilian aerospace to telecommunication and computer equipment. So Europe will be as disinclined to cede the region to the United States as the United States will be to welcome Europe into it as a strategic actor.

The most recent manifestation of the creeping emergence of such triangular politics is the ongoing trans-Atlantic debate about the EU efforts to lift its arms export embargo on China. In spring 2004, French and German leaders noted publicly that the embargo is an anachronism and should be abandoned. French leaders have since repeatedly reiterated their support for lifting the arms ban. Some officials even cited China's "improving" human rights credentials as proof that China had changed and the embargo was outdated. Chinese leaders, as part of their "year of Europe" diplomatic charm campaign, pressed European policymakers to drop the export ban, noting that it was an important step for China and the EU to solidify their recently annunciated "strategic partnership." The U.S. response was swift. U.S. policymakers lobbied their EU counterparts--especially Ireland, the president of the EU--to not vote on lifting the embargo. The United States also dispatched teams of military experts to EU capitals to sensitize them to China's military modernization efforts and the dangers posed by improving China's access to critical military technologies. Regardless of the understandable political motive of EU leaders, abandoning the embargo at a time when China-Taiwan tensions are high and when the possibility of armed conflict is real would, in American eyes, send the wrong signal to China and undermine cross-Strait stability. A European Council vote on the embargo was deferred in late March 2004, but the issue remains alive and is ripe for exacerbating U.S.-EU tensions.

Beyond the specifics of the China arms embargo debate and resulting tensions in trans-Atlantic relations, such triangular dynamics may not inevitably become the main driver of American or European policy toward China. There is much more that the United States and Europe share than either shares with the PRC. They have largely common values and global interests, are both advanced information-age democracies, have had a successful formal alliance for over half a century, and are prepared, more often than not, to use force on one another's behalf. In addition, the United States and Europe share basic hopes regarding China's future: to see it continue to join the international community as a responsible major power, a reliable economic partner, and a state moving inexorably toward pluralism and democracy. Nor do American and European policy aims diverge significantly on any of the key issues in East Asia: North Korea's denuclearization, peaceful resolution of the Taiwan dispute, and a stable and prosperous Southeast Asia.

In addition, Europe's own development and outlook limit the possibility of a triangular relationship with China and the United States. For Europeans, power--as defined by military means, by sovereignty over high-technology, and to some extent by the possibility to influence outcomes at the United Nations--remains vested at the national level and will remain so for the predictable future. In contrast, China is an aspiring great power and a veteran of great-power games. However, it faces tight limits on its freedom to maneuver: economic integration, and thus external dependence, for continued growth; underdeveloped military capacities; and soft points, such as the unresolved issue of sovereignty over Taiwan, concerns about Southeast Asia--e.g., Indonesian stability--and of course North Korea, for which the United States holds China mainly responsible.

This leaves only the United States with viable options to exercise genuine leverage over China and East Asia's strategic future. A strong "China card" policy by the United States, relying on incentives and pressures, has obvious implications for China's other international relations, including those with Europe. If the United States is able to induce China to tailor its behavior to U.S. needs and to ignore others, Europeans will see themselves as potential losers in East Asia. Their response might be to strengthen their own relations with China--the other candidate, Japan, being too intimate with the United States. A mercantilist approach by the United States toward China, in which commercial deals are sought with a view toward political influence, would surely feed resentment among Europeans and make European strategic cooperation with the United States in East Asia a thankless policy. Meanwhile, seeking counterweights to U.S. influence and pressures, the Chinese are likely to play on growing European economic interests, perhaps even more so as the EU's common foreign and security policy acquires teeth.

Like the Chinese, Europeans face temptations to maneuver around the strong U.S. position. For instance, France's past arms sales to Taiwan exploited U.S. restraint. More recently, Asian allies of the United States have understood that they may get better terms on high-tech deals with the United States by welcoming European competition. Beyond such gambits, and in the absence of an Asian integration process that would mirror Europe's own, China could be seen by Europe as both a key potential partner in its own right, economic engine of the region, and gatekeeper of a greater European role in East Asia.

Ultimately, the potential for Euro-Sino-American triangulation stems mainly from the strong position of the United States--the superpower and most important actor in the calculus of both China and Europe. If China feels blocked by a perceived U.S. containment strategy, it may look to Europe to outflank the United States and gain room to rise. If Europe feels uneasy about U.S. unilateralism in the use of its unmatched power, as it has recently felt in the case of Iraq, or if it resents the use of American political power for economic gain--or economic power for political gain--it could look to China to help check the United States.

Chinese and European interests in partnership may be all the more plausible given that Russia is no longer much of a power nor is it an interesting partner for either one. The Chinese appreciate the importance and potential of their economy and will use this leverage to advance their position in power politics--such as to divide the United States and Europe--as long as doing so does not harm China's own economic interests. In turn, rivalry can have strategic implications if either Europe or the United States compromises common security interests in order to gain preferential economic treatment, such as by transferring especially sensitive technology to China.

Having said all this, we can observe that next to nothing has really come of Chinese or Europe, especially French, experimentation with great-power multipolarity, as noted at the very beginning of this study. Conditions have not been auspicious: The post-Tiananmen sanctions have imposed a general restraint. After 9/11, both Europe and China (and Russia) rallied behind U.S. leadership in counterterrorism, albeit for their own counterterrorism reasons. Then, over Iraq, Europe divided itself on whether to support U.S. policy, while China, ostensibly critical, used its restraint to regain lost ground with the United States. Instead of advancing on the fertile ground of unpopular moves by the United States, multipolarity has receded as a practical option. So far, there has been no proof-of-principle of Chinese-European collaboration to balance or affect the United States, yet. At the same time, American overtures to China over Korea and Taiwan and a deemphasizing of human rights make current U.S. policy toward China closer to European policies.

None of this may matter much if China's evolution quickens on the path to a normal market democracy--that is, if its internal political development catches up with its economic rise. A debate is ongoing in today's China on what constitutes a peaceful path toward becoming a global power. But this cannot be taken for granted. If China emerges as a disruptive actor (in U.S. eyes) in Asian and world politics, the United States may shift its China policy away from engagement to containment or, more realistically, "constrainment." Whether or not such a U.S. strategy would be justified or efficacious, the Chinese might feel compelled to tack in turn. Although China could be steered by the United States into a helpful stance on East Asian and wider issues, it might instead feel a need to defy the United States and bypass U.S. obstacles in China's path in order to assert and exercise the independence that befits a great power.

In this context, the role of Europe could be significant. To the extent that Europe offers China economic, political, and even security cooperation, or possibly hope for any of these, the Chinese would be less likely to moderate their policies, the ability of the United States to constrain and dissuade China would be diminished, and the probability of Sino-American confrontation would rise. Moreover, Europe would be able to exploit to its economic advantage any effort by the United States to condition its economic cooperation on Chinese strategic behavior.

The other important side of the triangle is, of course, the U.S.-European one. As noted, the United States and Europe have substantial, closely aligned interests vis-à-vis China, and they remain, even after Iraq, international security partners. They may see merit in intensifying their cooperation in regard to China, pooling their resources and coordinating their positions for maximum affect on China and on shared U.S.-European interests that China has the potential to affect. They have ample coordinating mechanisms to do so. However, when it comes to China, there are important asymmetries between the United States and Europe. First, the United States has considerably greater ability than Europe to influence Chinese behavior and may, therefore, conclude that it has less to gain than Europe does from strategic coordination vis-à-vis China. Second, given the state of U.S.-European relations, Europe may be the more likely of the two to be enticed by China to pursue policies aimed at constraining the third power. Lastly, because of its security responsibilities in East Asia, the United States has more to lose than Europe if China's behavior is not influenced. Consequently, the United States has less to gain from cooperating with Europe vis-à-vis China, and Europe has more to gain from cooperating with China to the disadvantage of the United States.

Yet, in the final analysis, the authors believe that the advantages of pursuing common U.S.-European interests vis-à-vis China outweigh any gains that might come to either from seeking an exclusive, preferential, or manipulative relationship. The United States and Europe should not let their differences or competition regarding China give the weakest of the three powers the chance to play them against one another. From this perspective, the United States has more to lose than to gain by excluding Europe from its strategy toward China, and Europe has more to lose than to gain by trying to exploit U.S. efforts to temper China.

To the degree that this reasoning prevails over triangular temptations, several principles regarding U.S.-European policy coordination on China follow:

- The United States should not presume that it alone can or should influence Chinese strategy and behavior. It should view Europe as an asset and partner, not a follower, in a strategy to deal with China's rise and integration.

- Europe should take care not to give China reason to believe that any reckless international behavior would be regarded with less alarm by Europe than by the United States or, worse, that European sympathy would permit China to ignore U.S. policy.

- Neither the United States nor Europe should let otherwise healthy commercial competition weaken their joint efforts to achieve their common goal of integrating China and to advance and protect their common interests in East Asia.

These principles should be applied in several concrete issue areas:

- **Taiwan**: Any daylight between Europe and the United States on Chinese use of force would be dangerous; ideally, Europe should signal that it would provide physical support if Taiwan needed to be defended.
- **Korea**: Obviously, the Chinese need to feel constant pressure to twist North Korea's arm. That pressure should come from both Europe and the United States.
- **Southeast Asia**: Continued Chinese moderation toward the South China Sea and Southeast Asia generally, despite instabilities in that region, should be encouraged by both Atlantic powers.
- **Human rights**: The Chinese would take note of any difference in European and American attitudes on the treatment of human beings, and they might even try to reward the more understanding of the two.
- **Proliferation**: The Chinese should be disabused of any impression that Europeans are more relaxed than the Americans about WMD and missile proliferation.
- **World Trade Organization**: Intellectual property and other issues involving China should be common cause for the two co-leaders of the world trading system.

- **Arms sales**: The Chinese know they cannot get adequate advanced military systems from Russia, and their own military industrial base is technologically weak. If and as Chinese military modernization expands, the United States and Europe could easily be driven apart over American security concerns and European commercial opportunities.
- **High-technology markets**: the United States should not seek to extract total compliance from Europeans on their restraints to technology transfers while using its political influence to deny legitimate markets to the same Europeans.

This is not to suggest that the United States and Europe are headed for a clash over China. Instead, their respective policies are loosely in sync. But looking ahead, opportunities may arise for them to fall dangerously out of sync. Whether in the particulars or in the large, it is essential to get U.S.-European cooperation on China right for a simple reason: the world-shaping significance of China's rise.

There is an obvious U.S.-European bargain to be struck: Europe should not undercut the United States and the United States should not exclude Europe in dealing with the emergence of China. It is not enough for the United States simply to consult with Europe about China. It must be receptive to fashioning at least loosely common policies, even if they are shaded by the need to earn genuine European cooperation. In turn, by undercutting the United States, Europe would in effect be undercutting itself. And by virtue of gaining European support for a common approach, the United States would have every incentive to harness Europe's clout--its growing clout--to affect Chinese behavior for the good.

As suggested at the beginning of this study, China is increasingly active in regional and world affairs--by beginning to play the role of a great power--and in cooperating with the United States and others on such important security issues as terrorism and proliferation. At the same time, China is intensifying its military modernization, with a view toward improved area-denial capabilities vis-à-vis U.S. power-projection forces. While the Chinese do not appear to be committed to a strategy of countering U.S. power politically and militarily, they are evidently determined to invest as needed in China's military capabilities to deny the United States the ability dictate the terms of East Asian security, including the status of Taiwan.

There is no contradiction in this combination of a relatively accommodating foreign policy and stepped-up military modernization. But it does suggest that the Chinese are keeping open two strategic options:

- Follow a helpful approach toward the United States and the West until the military balance is less unfavorable to China.
- Deepen and expand cooperation with the West for the long term, while improving Chinese forces as insurance against military or political vulnerability.

Roughly stated, the first option is consistent with the logic of power politics, in which countering American hegemony is of paramount importance. The second option suggests recognition by the Chinese of the value of advancing shared interests through cooperative policies, largely irrespective of relative power positions.

Although the United States looms much larger than Europe, or any other power, in Chinese calculations, European policies can affect whether the Chinese lean toward the first or second of these two strategic options. To the extent that the Chinese believe that Europe is sympathetic toward the need to balance and constrain U.S. power, they may be more likely to indulge in such thinking themselves. If, instead, they see the United States and Europe coordinating their policies on matters of common interest, from the Middle East to global issues to China itself, the Chinese themselves may be more likely to see the advantages of cooperation, not merely for now but for the long haul.

APPENDIX
MEETING PARTICIPANTS AND AGENDA

LIST OF PARTICIPANTS

Marc Abensour	Deputy Director for North-East, Directorate for Asia and Oceania, French MoFA
Peter Almquist	Foreign Affairs Specialist, Strategic Transition Office, Arms Control Bureau, U.S. State Department
Stéphanie Balme	Research Fellow, CÉRI (International Studies and Research Center, Paris)
Amaya Bloch-Lainé	Director, Paris Office Program Officer, Marshall Memorial Fellowship, The German Marshall Fund of the U.S.
Sophie Boisseau du Rocher	Research Associate, Centre Asie Ifri
Jean-Pierre Cabestan	Director, French Center for Research on Contemporary China; Chief Editor, China Perspectives
Hervé Dejean de la Bâtie	Deputy Director for Asia and Oceania, French MoFA
Emmanuelle Delmer	China Analyst, Directorate for Asia and Oceania, French MoFA
Thérèse Delpech	Director for Strategic Affairs, Atomic Energy Council
Catherine Droszewski	China Analyst, International and Strategic Affairs, SGDN (National Defense General Secretariat), Paris
Christile Drulhe	Research Assistant, Centre Asie Ifri
Jean Esmein	Senior Research Fellow, CEREM (Multinational Business Study and Research Center), University Paris X--Nanterre
General Henri Eyraud (Rtd)	Former Defense Attaché in Beijing
François Godement	Director, Centre Asie Ifri, Paris
David Gompert	Emeritus Vice President, RAND Corporation
Christian Lechervy	Deputy Director for South-East Asia, Directorate for Asia and Oceania, French MoFA
Didier Leroy	Head of the Asia-Pacific Bureau, Directorate for Strategic Issues, French MoD
Radm. Michael McDevitt	Director, Center for Strategic Studies, Center for Naval Analyses Corporation
Evan Medeiros	Associate Political Scientist, RAND Corporation
James Mulvenon	Deputy Director, Center for Asia-Pacific Studies, RAND Corporation
Valérie Niquet	Director of Research, Institute of International and Strategic Relations (IRIS), Paris
Marianne Péron-Doise	Asia Analyst, Delegation for Strategic Affairs, French MoD

Arnaud Roux	China Office, Directorate for Asia and Oceania, French MoFA
Nicolas Ruble	Development Manager, International Crisis Group, Paris Office
Guillaume Schlumberger	Deputy Director, Exploitation of Technologies, Delegation for Strategic Affairs, French MoD
Régine Serra	Project Coordinator, Research Fellow, Centre Asie Ifri
Bruno Tertrais	Senior Research Fellow, Foundation for Strategic Research (FRS)
Gregory Treverton	Senior Policy Analyst, RAND Corporation
Frank Umbach	Senior Research Fellow, German Council on Foreign Relations (DGAP), Berlin, Germany

AGENDA

June 24, 2003

19:30--21:30   Informal dinner with U.S. participants
Restaurant 'Le Regnier,' 58 rue Dutot, Paris 15 (near the Holiday Inn Hotel)

June 25, 2003

9:30   **Opening Session**

Francois Godement, Director, Centre Asie Ifri
David Gompert, Emeritus Vice President, RAND Corporation
Thérèse Delpech, Director for Strategic Affairs, Atomic Energy Council

9:45   **Presentation of the pre-report**

'China's Current Cooperative Strategy: Tactical or Strategic Shift?'

François Godement, Director, Centre Asie Ifri
David Gompert, Emeritus Vice President, RAND Corporation
Evan Medeiros, Associate Political Scientist, RAND Corporation
James Mulvenon, Political Scientist, RAND Corporation

11:00   Coffee break

12:15   Lunch at Ifri

13:30   General Debate

17:00   End of Seminar